To Rome With Love

A Study In The Book of Romans, Part Two
By Anne Nicholson

Copyright © 2021 Anne Nicholson

All rights reserved. No part of this book may be reproduced by any means, graphic, electronic, or mechanical, including photocopying, recording, taping or by and information storage retrieval system without the written permission of the author except in the case of brief quotations embodied in critical articles and reviews.

Scripture taken from the New King James Version®, Copyright © 1982 by Thomas Nelson.
Used by permission. All rights reserved.

THE HOLY BIBLE, NEW INTERNATIONAL VERSION®, NIV® Copyright © 1973, 1978, 1984, 2011 by Biblica, Inc. ®
Used by permission. All rights reserved worldwide.

Scripture taken from the Amplified Bible, Copyright © 1954, 1958, 1962, 1964, 1965, 1987 by The Lockman Foundation.
Used with permission.

Books may be ordered through booksellers or by contacting:
Open Heavens Publishing
1369 Burke Lane
Auburn, AL 36830
www.ohministry.com
anne@ohministry.com
334.329.4142

Because of the dynamic nature of the Internet, any web addresses or links contained in this book may be changed since publication and may no longer be valid. The views expressed in this work are solely those of the author and do not necessarily reflect the views of the publisher, and the publisher hereby disclaims any responsibility for them.

Any people depicted in stock imagery provided by Getty Images are models,
and such images are being used for illustrative purposes only.

Certain stock imagery © Getty Images.

Print Version: ISBN: 978-1-9537-4207-0
Library of Congress Control Number: 2021905962
Kindle Version: ISBN: 978-1-9537-4211-7
Library of Congress Control Number: 2021914560

Print information available on the last page.
Open Heavens Publishing rev. date: August 15, 2021

List of Weekly Lessons and Scriptures

A Continuation Of The Redeemed And What We Believe
Romans Chapters 8 - 11

C. Freedom from Sin's Grasp (Continued): Righteousness Imparted – Sanctification

#		
#11	**Romans 1-7**	A Review of Romans 1-7
#12	**Romans 8:1-17**	Life Through The Power Of The Holy Spirit
#13	**Romans 8:18-39**	Future Glory & More Than Conquerors

D. God's Righteousness Vindicated: The Justice of God & Israel's Past, Present & Future

#14	**Romans 9**	God's Sovereign Choice & Israel's Unbelief
#15	**Romans 10**	The Jew's Rejection Of Christ
#16	**Romans 11**	Restoration: The Remnant Of Israel & Engrafted Branches

Part II: The Redeemed and How We Behave
Romans Chapters 12 - 16

E. Righteousness Practiced: Finishing Strong In Christ

#17	**Romans 12**	Living Sacrifices - Vessels Of Love
#18	**Romans 13**	Submission To Authorities & Loving Like Christ
#19	**Romans 14**	Finding Unity In The Love of Christ
#20	**Romans 15**	Paul's Closing Summation
#21	**Romans 16**	Paul's Commendation, Greetings, & Doxology

Introduction

Greetings!

Welcome to Part Two of a study in the book of Romans. Together, we are embarking on a remarkable journey to embrace the love, liberty, and grace of this most beloved Epistle. Theologians have called it the most important letter ever written. That should make us all sit up and take notice! Let me say that again; it has been called the most significant letter ever written. Think about that for a minute. Since the beginning of the written word, millions, possibly billions of love letters have been written, but this is it. Romans is #1, even today. It is timeless, and its powerful message still eclipses the great works of literary giants like Shakespeare, Emerson, and Tolstoy. Why? Although penned by Paul through the inspiration of the Holy Spirit, its author is God. We know from scripture that God is love, and that's His overarching message in Romans. He loves you, and He has a plan for you. He always had a plan to save you!

The letter is so powerful, perfect, and complete that theologians have agreed if this Epistle were all you had of scripture, you would have enough. You would have more than enough to come to an understanding of not only who God is, and in light of that who you are, but also an understanding of God's plan to save sinners. Through the inspired text, you will discover that God is eternal and well as His plan. Because of His infinite love, He's always had a plan to save you. He's loved you from eternity past, and that's not as you should be, but just as you are.

Infinite Love.

Wouldn't you like to understand God's amazing love in a intimate or personal way? Through the study, you can. You'll be invited to practice His presence and embrace His Words as you come to a fuller understanding of His infinite, complete, and holy love for you. From Paul's soothing words, you'll see the depth of God's faithful love and feel His embrace. Think about it! The one and only true God - the creator of heaven and earth - loves you!

But those words don't do it justice. It's much more than love as we know it. At this very moment, His love for you is absolute. It's whole! It's not at all like human love, which can be fickle and unfaithful. God's love is so accomplished and complete that you can't affect it. You can't do anything good or bad or different or better to cause God to love you more than He already does and already has. You're about to discover that while you were a sinner and a God-hater, running after everything this world could offer – and away from Him - God loved you, even still, and died for you. Now, I ask you, "How profound is that?"

Paul got this, and no place in scripture is it more clearly defined than in Romans. If understanding His love weren't enough, every element of the profound theological works of God are navigated, explored, and explained in Romans. Paul also outlines and establishes God's plan for Israel, the chosen people of God. The text settles questions like, "What will happen to the Jews?" Finally, Paul draws his letter to a close by outlining the right and acceptable Christian living. He makes it simple and concise. Paul tells it like it is. He implores us to come into agreement with God and finish strong in a way that brings honor and glory to the name Jesus because, above all else - it benefits the gospel.

Make It A Personal Journey.

I want to encourage you to make this study a personal journey. Approach each lesson and biblical text prayerfully, as if Paul's letter was written just to you. Although the message does not omit one element of fundamental doctrine, the overarching theme is love. Through Romans, God's love for humanity, the pinnacle of His creation, His image-bearers, and purveyors of love, hope, and truth on the earth come to light. Historically, Romans is identified as the believer's Declaration of Independence. It's also our biblical Constitution and Bill of Rights. In short, its 16 chapters consisting of 9,447 words rightly teach, affirm, and define what we believe and why we believe it. It's God's plan – not man's. In light of that knowledge, Romans teaches us how all believers should behave.

The esteemed Epistle has been melting the hearts of men since Phoebe delivered it from Corinth to the church of Rome in 57 AD. Although she is not singled out for this service in scripture, many biblical scholars believe that she was its courier. If so, this would make her the only woman to deliver an original biblical text to its recipients. Be encouraged and take note of this. Throughout history, God has called, anointed, and equipped women to be His vessels and servants – agents of His Holy Word.

If Paul were with us today, and you asked him to name his most significant work, he would no doubt confess the book of Romans. Through the centuries, its inspired words have birthed every great awakening of the church. Noted theologians, men like Irenaeus, Augustine, Martin Luther, Karl Barth, George Muller, John and Charles Wesley, David Brainerd, and countless others have been so moved and inspired by its text that each was ushered into a heightened revelation of God's grace and perfect plan to save sinners. When its life-changing words take root in a heart, everything else pales in comparison. With meaning and divine purpose, we see vividly that salvation from start to finish is a holy and sacred work of God. It's always been a work of the Trinity.

It's All About God.

Reading and studying Romans brings God front and center because the revelation of Christ shapes every chapter and verse. It gives us the profound opportunity to know the God who loves us, calls us, and saves us - personally. Moreover, it gives us purpose to pause and reflect on His righteousness and our created need for Him. Ladies, we need God, and Jesus will meet us in every verse. So, anticipate Him! We will genuinely delight to worship, adore, and praise our great God and King – Jesus through its pages.

In closing, remember this. *To Rome With Love* is your study in Romans. Make it what you will. As we travel this road together, it is my hopeful prayer that our collective lives will never be the same. Together, we can finish strong, walking in liberty and loving like Christ until the end. It will take commitment and perseverance. Each lesson will require a minimum commitment of 30 minutes. If you're not inclined to follow through, I encourage you to ask someone to be your accountability partner. That's an investment that will benefit you and those you love all the days of your life.

I can promise you that! Make a plan to get alone with God and pray for wisdom, insight, and clarity as you study. As you conclude each lesson, pray for transformation. Ask Jesus for the grace to come into agreement with God's Word and seal it in your heart. Then walk in grace and believing faith that His Holy Spirit will bring His Word to performance in your life. Sisters, He Will Do It! Be blessed as you study! I will be praying for you.

Love and Blessings,
Anne

Note: Unless otherwise indicated, all scripture is taken from the NKJV. Scripture taken from the New King James Version®. Copyright © 1982 by Thomas Nelson. Used by permission. All rights reserved.

All calligraphy by Kate Gwin @ www.haintbluecollective.com

About The Study Guide

The Romans study is designed to promote reflection and prayer, confession, liberation, and response. Weekly, your higher purpose is to understand God's Word and come into agreement with it. The weekly format is outlined below.

Day One - **Read.** Day One introduces the week's passages through a series of questions designed to grow us in knowledge, understanding, right living, and the will and purposes of God. Every week, the overarching question is: "What does God say?"

Day Two - **Research.** You will Identify, investigate, and define ***keywords*** and ***key phrases*** in the week's text that provide foundational doctrine elements. Romans is full of words and passages that we must know, understand, and embrace. We don't want to miss out on their dominant meaning or application. Words such as justification, sanctification, glorification, etc., will be examined. Additionally, difficulties in the text will be pinpointed, studied, and recommended for further group discussion.

Day Three - **Receive.** You are called to agree with God's Word. Our Lord desires that you open your heart to receive His truth, remembering that God's living word renews your mind as it washes over you and is empowered by the Holy Spirit. (See Romans 12:2.) As you agree with God, your soul finds spiritual refreshing and satisfaction.

Day Four - **Reflect**. You're invited to examine your heart and motives in light of God's Word. While examining the text, you will ask and answer, "What is God speaking to me?" "Do I have an accurate understanding of God's Word in these passages?" "Is change needed in my life?"

Day Five - **Respond.** As you respond, you'll walk in the liberty and victory of transformation. You are ready to embrace the world around you. That always begins in a humble setting among those who know you best and love you anyway - your family and real friends. With a liberated and joyful heart, you will be challenged to bring your behavior and attitude in line with your confession of faith. Fully embracing God's truth, you have the unprecedented honor and privilege of imitating Christ. Rejoice, today you respond by moving forward in the strength of the Holy Spirit to righteous living and loving like Jesus!

A Word Of Encouragement.

No one ever studied God's Word and remained the same, particularly the epistle to the Romans. This beloved, life-changing revelation of Christ is challenging, liberating, and inspirational. It is my opinion that if you marinated only in Romans for your remaining days, you could finish strong, transformed, and completely satisfied.

Each week highlights passages that have spoken expressly to my heart. Look for them! They are ♥ <u>**Heart-Check For Today**</u>. Each lesson will include a memory verse. Please commit it to prayer.

You will be invited to journal or write a prayer that reveals what God's Spirit is speaking to you from the selected passages from time to time. I hope you enjoy the journey. You're in for an incredible spiritual transformation.

Lesson 11: A Review of Romans 1 - 7

Day One: **Read**

Romans' Theme Verse: "For I am not ashamed of the gospel of Christ, for it is the power of God to salvation for everyone who believes, for the Jew first and also for the Greek. For in it the righteousness of God is revealed from faith to faith; as it is written, 'The just shall live by faith' " (Romans 1:16-17).

As the saints of old would agree, Romans 1 – 7 proved to be more than a challenge. It not only prompted an awakening; it was a life-changing journey as well. That's why this lesson is so important. Since Romans builds upon a foundation that began in its first chapter, and since you're looking for a strong finish, it's crucial to highlight and review what we covered in part one of our studies. Therefore, we'll begin part two with several significant questions.

As a result of your study in Romans, are you looking more like Jesus?

And second, are you living by faith alone - in Christ alone?

What's the core of both issues? Simply this. "How has your heart been changed through the study of Romans?" To settle these matters, let's begin our review.

In **Lessons 1 – 4,** humanity's need for God was exposed. All of us - everyone who has lived, now lives, or will live in the future - needs God. Our need goes back to the very beginning, back to *"In the beginning God..." (Genesis 1:1)*. These lessons expose humanity's universal unrighteousness from our inception. We've pushed against God from the Garden of Eden. In so doing, our human condition was revealed. Surprisingly, it surfaced in a place of unprecedented peace and tranquility, a place where Adam and Eve enjoyed fellowship with God. Not just ordinary fellowship, either. They enjoyed His divine presence as He strolled through the garden in the cool of the day. Although God had provided all they needed, including Him, they wanted more. Their desire to push against God and go their way indicates our ancestors were not only helpless but willful and stubborn too. Although they had all they could ever need, they weren't satisfied. How utterly human! So, as you can see, we were doomed right from the beginning.

Right off the bat, Paul exposed our great need for God. You will recognize that need because Paul takes great pains to make it abundantly clear. There will be no misunderstanding; we are all without excuse because even nature reveals God's unique and infinite glory. With piercing eloquence, Paul contrasts and compares God's righteousness in light of humanity's unrighteousness. That sets the tone for the entire book. We all need God – pure and simple.

Lesson One not only introduced you to sin and unrighteousness but to Paul as well. He is the one who received inspiration from God to write the beloved Epistle. This lesson also highlights Romans' thesis or theme passage. All sixteen chapters will support and confirm the powerful words of Romans 1:16-17. As you begin, you will want to review those passages.

In **Lesson Two**, Paul explained God's wrath against humanity. He began by highlighting the Gentiles. So that you know, that's everyone who is not born Jewish. Note that God's wrath was against the sin in man, not man - personally. God loves the sinner but hates all sin. After all, sin nailed Jesus to the cross. God was serious about sin, then, as He is now. Even though times have changed, God's position about sin has not. He still hates sin and cannot be in its presence, nor will He overlook sin or condone it.

Moreover, sin kills! It leads to death, spiritually and naturally. Too, it separates you from God, which is in direct opposition to His purpose in creating you – for fellowship. In Paul's assault against sin, he contrasts it with God's love as he brings sin's deadly outcome to light. "For the wages of sin is death, but the gift of God is eternal life in Christ Jesus our Lord" (Romans 6:23). Look at the contrast. God made a way – the only way. In love, He sent Jesus to save us! Romans 6:23 assures us, we have life in Christ Jesus, but sin leads to death. Keep in mind that we are not talking about believers' sins that are quickly confessed and turned from through repentance. Paul is referencing all habitual, unrepentant, and unconfessed sin or sin as a lifestyle. He called out habitual sinners, people who live far from God and reject His grace and forgiveness. That would be those who disregard Him altogether and say in their foolish hearts, "There is no God!" Instead, these have made themselves, or others, their God. Shamefully, they are bent toward worshiping the creature rather than the Creator.

In **Lesson Three**, Paul outlined the Jews' relationship to the law – after all, they were its original recipients. Additionally, Paul defined God's righteous judgment, which is always perfect, fair, and just. The Jews had no excuse, they were not only God's chosen, but they had every opportunity to acknowledge God and turn to Him. Paul reminds us that everywhere – all around us - nature declares the glory of God and confirms His existence. They were given ample opportunity to acknowledge God and praise and worship Him. Their ancestors had seen first-hand the mighty power of God. Tragically, many exchanged the truth of God for a lie and lived in sin. With hardened hearts, they rejected love, a love that could save them. Instead, they defiantly turned their backs on God.

Since that was the case, next, Paul laid out the depravity of humanity in **Lesson Four**. His conclusion? We are without excuse – every last one of us. We're all guilty – as guilty as guilty can be. Mercifully, He won't leave us in our hopeless state. We owe our thanks to God. He had a plan, and it was to save us. It was to save you. You are saved because it was God's perfect plan from eternity past. That's long before the foundation of the world. Because God loves you, it was always His plan to save you.

Beginning with **Lesson Five**, Paul introduced a new concept – righteousness by grace through faith. What good news! That means although you're as guilty as guilty can be, as are we, you enjoy the righteousness of Jesus before a Holy God because you have believed. Christ's righteousness has been imputed to you. That means it is attributed or credited to your spiritual account. That spiritual transaction occurred the moment you came to faith. You can't earn it, and you can't buy it. Believing is the only way to salvation – on purpose. God has intentionally done the heavy lifting. He has prepared the way because we could never make it on our own. Think about it. If you could earn your salvation, how would you know that you had done enough? Since some of us are born "doers," and others are born "doubters," we'd exhaust ourselves and still not be certain. Mercifully, God has lightened our load. Regardless of how you might be feeling, remember this. Faith is not linked to a feeling. Instead, it's bound to a faithful God who declares faith is *"...the substance of things hoped for, the evidence of things not seen"* (See Hebrews 11:1). You are saved the moment you believe.

God's plan is ideal. It involves no work, that's why some people miss it. They can't reconcile the fact that it's based on belief - pure and simple. Since salvation from start to finish belongs to God and requires nothing of us, other than believing, they assume it can't be real. But it's true! It's never been about what we could do. Instead, it's about what God has done on our behalf. All you need to do is believe. God promises that "everyone who calls upon the name of the Lord shall be saved." (See Romans 10:13 and Acts 2:21.) There are no qualifiers in these verses – no, not one. What good news! That means anyone - anywhere - throughout history is saved and justified by faith, not works. Everyone who believes is declared not guilty in the eyes of a Holy God simply because they put their faith in His Son's atoning work on Calvary. Graciously, God has prepared the way. It's Jesus! The work is complete – it is finished. Salvation has always been God's work, and we receive its benefits by faith alone.

Lesson Six covered Romans 5, which highlights our end game. Even if you've never considered it, you will spend eternity somewhere – either heaven or hell. That's an appointment that all of us will keep because these bodies are perishable. Your "tent" is not only growing older - it's getting more and more worn with each passing year. But thanks to Jesus, we can look forward to being with Him forever. You are promised everlasting life! Eternity with Him is part of God's plan. It is an eschatological victory and a benefit of salvation. One day, you will see the glory of the Son as we stand in His presence. Just think - you will not only be with Jesus - you will be like Jesus, too. He is the one who loved you with an everlasting love and could cover your sins. Because of His plan from eternity past, you will live forever!

Paul began **Lesson Seven** by declaring that we are dead to sin and alive in Christ. The "old man" – our old sin nature - has been put to death. It died with Christ on Calvary, and you were raised in Christ with His resurrection. You need not fear – you've got this because the mighty grip of God holds you. He will see you through. This sanctification will take a lifetime. Although it's been promised, it will not be complete this side of heaven. Nonetheless, you have cause to rejoice! When you stand before Jesus, His work will be complete. (See Philippians 1:6).

Next, Paul began to teach about the freedom you have in Christ Jesus. How exciting? When you come to faith, you have freedom from sin and sin's grip. Paul guarantees that you can be free from sin's grasp because Christ's righteousness has been imparted (conveyed, given) to you. You have Christ in you – the hope of glory. Book Two picks up where you left off. You will prayerfully consider right living in light of your positional righteousness in Christ Jesus.

Lessons Eight identified us as slaves to righteousness. Is that a fair description of you? We are spiritually righteous because the transaction has already occurred. It was finished at the cross. But, as the redeemed – His bride, His Church – how do you live? Do you pursue righteousness? Do you think and do what is honoring to Jesus? Do you have a longing in your heart to be like Jesus and be with Jesus?

Paul didn't stop there. As Christ's bride and part of His Church, **Lesson Nine** focused on marriage. How fitting! After all, you are His beloved! Is Jesus yours? Are you looking for His return? Search your heart. Only you can answer these questions. Bear in mind; we won't get it perfect here. Not in this life. The crucial question becomes, "Is Jesus truly Lord of your life?" That's where the real work is accomplished, deep within each heart. It occurs when you acknowledge the truth about God, agree with His Word and respond accordingly.

So then, an overarching question becomes: "Who is God, and what's that to me?" Ladies, that question is as old as time. You either believe that God is who He says He is, or you don't. And guess what? What you believe or think about God not only shapes your eternal destiny – your future – but it shapes today as well. What you believe about God always surfaces in the way you do life. How so? It's revealed in relationships. It's declared in your home life, through your marriage, and in your child-rearing. If you work outside your home, it's also seen in the workplace. Truthfully, it's evidenced at all times and in all places. Living to righteousness truly matters. You are His witness! Lest you forget, people are watching and looking for evidence that God is real. They are looking for a reason to believe that Jesus lived to die for sinners – everywhere – including them! Your life, consistently yielded to Him, could be all a family member, co-worker, or neighbor needs to come to faith – authentic saving faith. That's believing that God is real, loves them, and died for their sins too.

Paul wrapped it all up in **Lesson Ten** as we examined humanity's struggle with sin. We faced humanity's struggle head-on because it's an issue for all of us. Even Paul struggled with sin – sometimes. He confessed it. If Paul struggled, how much more shall we? Ladies, I told you before, "It ain't heaven yet." We live in a sinful world – and sinful people surround us.

Moreover, you live in a body that is tainted with sin. Your spirit and flesh continually push against one another. You are at war; it's a battle! Sin will be part of your life until you see Jesus face to face. Only then will that struggle end. Nevertheless, Paul encourages us to get up each day and live right because we are right! Another theologian said: "You are right, so be right!"

The truth of the matter is this. Every day you have the opportunity to aim for perfection. You won't succeed, but with your eye on the prize – that's Jesus – you will get closer to the goal you're desiring. What's that? Living lives that glorify God and point people to Jesus. As you go about your daily life, you can put God first, others second, and yourself last. Believers should endeavor to out-kind one another and not only speak of love but live it out. After all, we are His hands and feet and His only purveyors of love, hope, and peace on the earth.

In closing, you have a choice – every day. You can live to righteousness; Paul said it's doable. You can purpose in your heart each day to live a life that honors God. It won't be mistake-free. King David's wasn't either. Yet, he loved God with all his heart, and that's what God saw – not his frail humanity. You must remember this. Even though you're not going to be perfect here, it's already accomplished in the spiritual sense. Rejoice! You are perfect in God's sight. When God looks at you, He sees Jesus.

In the future, you are encouraged to get up each day and embrace your justification as you live by faith. You are the beloved's, and He is yours! You owe all your thanks to God. Salvation has always been by faith alone in Christ alone. And thankfully, that will never change.

Lesson 11: A Review of Romans 1-7

Day Two: **Research**.

I. Using a dictionary, bible dictionary, or concordance define the following *keywords*.

gospel vv. 1:1, 9, 16

grace vv. 1:5, 7

sexual immorality v. 1:29

repentance v. 2:4

justified v. 3:24

redemption v. 3:24

II. Read the following *key phrases*:

obedience to the faith v. 1:5 - Saving faith always produces obedience and submission to Jesus Christ. We trust Him, we love Him, and we obey Him. Jesus said it plainly in John 14:15. Prayerfully record John 14:15 below.

John 14:15

♥ Heart-Check For Today

What's on your heart? Where is your Rome? Is there someplace that you are longing to share the good news? What about within your family? Paul had a kingdom focus, do you? Read Acts 1:8. It's the call of the global church. That means it's your call, too, because if you're saved, you're called! Prayerfully record Acts 1:8 below.

Record Acts 1:8

receiving in themselves the penalty of their error v. 1:27 - Our text reports that those choosing to engage in a perverse sexual activity receive the "due penalty" of their error. The Greek for "due penalty" is not talking about an unusual punishment from God. Instead, it emphasizes that those engaging in such sin will reap the consequence which is natural and logical to their actions. As God's created beings, His image-bearers, we cannot violate the natural use of our bodies without consequences. The word "use" in verses 26 & 27 is *chrēsis* in Greek. The meaning of "use," according to the *Dictionary of Biblical Language: Greek New Testament and the Greek-English Lexicon of the NT*, "is *sexual function, sexual use.*" Note: It is crucial to understand there is no mention of "orientation, bent or inclination" in the original meaning of this word. Even though people argue that today, Paul merely stated a fact from God, all offenders were using (and use) their bodies outside the natural order and sexual function as designed by God. We cannot violate the natural use of our bodies and then blame God for the shameful or painful results. All sin has consequences. Paul said, "...the wages of sin is death..." (See Romans 6:23.) If we remain unrepentant, we will die in our sin. We will experience not only physical or natural death but spiritual death as well. Lest we forget, only the Redeemed of God will inherit His kingdom.

God gave them over v. 1:28 - This is a judicial term relating to judgment and the dispensing or administration of justice. In Greek, the term is used for handing over a prisoner to his sentence. When men consistently abandon God, there are painful consequences.

"And he went out to meet Asa, and said to him: 'Hear me, Asa, and all Judah and Benjamin. The LORD *is* with _____ while you are with _____. If you _____ Him, He will be _____ by you; but if you _____ Him, He will _____ _____ ' " (2 Chronicles 15:2).

turned aside v. 3:12 - "turned aside" means to lean in the wrong direction. One theologian likened its original meaning to describe a soldier running the wrong way or deserting. Referencing the *Greek-English Lexicon of the New Testament*, to turn aside, *"to avoid," to no longer put one's trust or confidence in someone—to turn away from (God). In essence, to veer off the path, to venture off course, to swerve."* From the beginning of time, man's natural inclination has been a departure from God's way while seeking after their own. Again, that was the root of the original sin. What's a sin? At its core, it's disobedience to God. Our definition is *"any failure to conform to the moral law of God in act, attitude, or nature."* So that we're clear concerning sin, that would include our <u>words, actions, and deeds, as well as our motives and intent</u>. (Emphasis added.) Complete Isaiah 53:6 below.

"All we like _____ have gone _____; we have turned, every _____, to his _____ way; And the Lord has laid on Him the _____ of us all" (Isaiah 53:6).

fear of God v. 3:18 - Biblical fear of God is a two-fold revelation linked to the nature and character of God. First, the revelation of God brings awe and wonder to the hearts of man. Next, that revelation is accompanied by a healthy, reverent fear of violating God's holy nature. In other words, to know Him is to love Him, to reverence Him, and to obey Him. Complete Proverbs 9:10 below.

"The _____ of the _____ is the beginning of _____, And the _____ of the _____ One is _____" (Proverbs 9:10).

an open tomb v. 13 - Literally, it was an open grave, which exposed or emitted the decay, disease, and stench of the deceased to passersby. Metaphorically speaking, "Their open throats, like tombs," revealed the condition of man's heart by allowing others (passersby) to smell the stench and decay of their cold dead hearts. Read Matthew 12:34. What does Jesus reveal about the origin of our words? Record the phrase below.

Note: Sin has not changed, nor will it. Sin is sin, and salvation is still salvation; furthermore, God's plan has not changed. Dr. Warren W. Wiersbe, author, and theologian stated: "There is no difference in the great message of Romans—no difference in sin (Romans 3:22–23) or salvation (Romans 10:12–13). God has regarded both Jew and Gentile as under sin that He might, in grace, have mercy upon all" (Romans 11:32).[1]

---

1   Wiersbe, W. W. (1992). *Wiersbe's expository outlines on the New Testament* (p. 370). Wheaton, IL: Victor Books.

Lesson 11: A Review of Romans 1-7

Day Three: **Receive.** Prayerfully Read Romans 3:9-20

Memory Verse: "They have all turned aside; They have together become unprofitable; There is none who does good, no, not one" (Romans 3:12).

As we begin a review of Romans 3:9-20, remember that God loves the sinner but hates all sin. In these verses, Paul discusses the depravity of humanity. It's a human condition that was thankfully settled at the cross. The only remedy for our unrighteous condition was, and is, a righteous King. That would be Jesus. He has not only won the victory over sin; He has conquered the grave as well. His work is finished.

As His child, you are secure. You have the surety of pardon and the guarantee of eternal life. He's your ticket in, and you have His Spirit inside! But it's much more than that. He will never leave you or forsake you. He will remain with you every moment of every day until the mountains melt like wax or until God calls you home. So you can rejoice! Jesus' righteousness is yours, and it's not circumstantial - it's absolute! And that's despite how you feel, what you've done, or where you've been. When you believed or came to faith, that authentic faith trumped everything else because you have placed your faith in Jesus. God sees you seated in heavenly places and established in the victory of the cross. A theologian of old said it like this. "When God looks at you, He sees you through the cross!"

Furthermore, God sees you in the future, not only with Jesus but like Him too. What excellent news! Although we still struggle with sin and sometimes feel weak, indeed, we have much cause to rejoice.

God's Glorious Plan.

God planned to save you before the world began. His plan was birthed in the Trinity by God the Father, God the Son, and God the Spirit. They determined to save you from eternity past, and then at the appointed time, Jesus was born to die. Lest we forget, although sins nailed Jesus to the cross, it was His love - God's love - that held Him there. In one gracious act, their great love consumed all the sins and evil in the world – past, present, and future. The cross of Calvary is where the love of God collided with the human condition called depravity. God has accomplished great things on your behalf. What is your debt of gratitude? What can you offer Him in return? Although He asks nothing, He desires your heart. You can love the Lord your God with all your heart, soul, mind, and strength. According to Jesus, that's the greatest commandment, and loving your neighbor as yourself is the second. Jesus concluded, "On these two commandments hang all the Law and the Prophets" (Matthew 22:40).

Moreover, since "the just shall live by faith," you can offer yourself as a living sacrifice to God. Looking forward, Paul will conclude Romans 11 (Lesson 16) with glorious praise to God, since all things are of Him, through Him and for Him. Paul points us to the truth, to Our Creator – God – who is the rightful end, source, and sustainer of everything that exists. In Hebrews 11, God highlighted faith and heroes of the faith. That's men and women who lived by faith and realized incredible victories in all types of circumstances and situations. How so? Because saving faith lives and moves after a pattern of God, as He so wills and guides, it carries us through. It accomplishes all things as "the just live by faith." In return, what is your reasonable service? As Paul said, it's merely this. "I beseech you therefore, brethren, by the mercies of God, that you present your bodies a living sacrifice, holy, acceptable to God, which is your reasonable service" (Romans 12:1).

With that thought in mind, let's pray. Before moving forward, take a few minutes to offer a prayer of thanksgiving to God. He alone is worthy of your praise. He has done great things for you.

1. Review Paul's summary statement of Romans 3:9. According to Paul, both the Jews and Greeks "are all under sin." Paul will substantiate his claim as we move through the lesson. With wisdom and accuracy, he reaches back into the Old Testament for confirmation through the inspired words of the psalmist. In so doing, he eloquently proves humanity's depraved condition by highlighting their predisposed temperament, natural bent, and inclination to sin. As we shall see, they were enslaved and dominated by sin. Incidentally, anyone who lives apart from Christ's righteousness remains the same. Read Romans 3:9 and record the last sentence of the verse below.

2. Read Psalm 14:1-3 and record the highlights from each verse.

v. 1

v. 2

v. 3

3. Now read and record the *similar words and phrases* from Psalm 53:1-3. Pay special attention to the last phrase of verses 1 and 3. Be sure to include these words in your answer.

v. 1

v. 2

v. 3

4. For reinforcement, review Psalm 14:1. Who says in his heart, "There is no God"?

5. Review Romans 3:10-18 below. **Underline** the words "none or not one" and **circle** the words "all, together" and "their/they" in these passages. These inclusive words reveal the nondiscriminatory evil of humanity's sin and rebellion. How many times does Paul use each group of words?

none; not one _____ all; together; their/they _____

As it is written:

"There is none righteous, no, not one;
There is none who understands;
There is none who seeks after God.
They have all turned aside;
They have together become unprofitable;
There is none who does good, no, not one."
"Their throat is an open tomb;
"With their tongues they have practiced deceit";
"The poison of asps is under their lips";
"Whose mouth is full of cursing and bitterness."
"Their feet are swift to shed blood;
Destruction and misery are in their ways;
And the way of pece they have not known."
"There is no fear of God before their eyes."

6. Review Romans 3:10-18. These verses expose and confirm their guilt. They also serve as an indictment of their (Jews and Greeks) character, conversation, and conduct. In your opinion, which verse(s) speak to the following:

their character:

their conversation:

their conduct:

Lesson 11: A Review of Romans 1-7

Day Four: **Reflect**. Prayerfully Read Romans 3:21-4

Memory Verse: "But to him who does not work but believes on Him who justifies the ungodly, his faith is accounted for righteousness..." (Romans 4:5).

Faith is everything because it saves us! Today's lesson will highlight God's grand plan for salvation through faith in Christ alone. Salvation comes to all who believe, to all who call upon the name Jesus. We find the surety of pardon and the promise of salvation repeatedly in scripture. Simply stated, all who believe will be saved. That's God's promise! Have you placed your hope in the One who promised? Like all promises, a faithful outcome is linked to the promiser. In this case, He's a faithful and loving God who cannot lie. He wants you to embrace this promise and believe in Jesus. He, alone, will see you through. Salvation is a spiritual work that is of God and from God. He created it, chooses its recipients, and oversees to their spiritual awakening or rebirth. He undergirds that faith throughout this life. Salvation is God's merciful gift and comes only by way of faith.

Thankfully, you can't earn it, buy it, or bring it about in your strength; it doesn't come through works. Paul said, "lest any man should boast." That's a good thing because how would you ever know you had done enough? Paul assured the church at Ephesus, *"For by grace you have been saved through faith, and that not of yourselves; it is the gift of God, not of works, lest anyone should boast" (Ephesians 2:8-9)*. Receiving salvation by grace through faith in Jesus, being wholly His - and forgiven - is humanity's ultimate gift.

If you're saved, you have believed in God's promise. Many years ago, God began to record a story about these people – His people who believed His promises and lived by faith. God, the creator of heaven and earth (and everything in it), chose them. He called or awakened them spiritually, enabling them to believe in Him. These hoped in what they could not see. That's faith, and it will never change. By biblical definition in Hebrews 11:1, we find that faith is *"the substance of things hoped for, the evidence of things not seen" [Emphasis added].* Although God was not visible, they hoped in His promise. That's radical – and it's faith. The man who first believed and walked by faith was Abraham, along with his wife, Sarah. He is, even still, the Father of Faith.

1. Today's lesson points us toward a hill called Calvary, but before Paul takes us there, his inspired words reach back into the Old Testament to outline the beginning of how "the just have lived by faith!" Review Romans 4:3 and complete the verse below.

"For what does the Scripture say? "_____ *believed* _____, *and it was* _____ to him for _____."

Beginning with Abraham, faith was not only identified and recorded in scripture; it was highlighted so we could see how it looks to believe and hope in things we cannot see – namely, God. In his and Sarah's journey, God called forth a nation and established a pattern and type of followers, the just (justified), who live by faith. It was a simple formula. God spoke, and Abraham listened; God guided, and Abraham moved; God promised, and Abraham believed. Although that's a simple explanation, it nicely sums up Abraham's faith-filled journey with God.

2. What was Abraham's call? Prayerfully read Genesis 12:1-9 and highlight the important facts from each verse.

v. 1

v. 2

v. 3

v. 4

v. 5

v. 6

v. 7

v. 8

v. 9

3. Regardless of how long you've been saved, all believers are on a faith journey with God. Although you may not think of it as such, ideally, that's what it is. God has plans for you; He is guiding your journey, too, and you can rest assured, it's far from over. Through the hardships or victories, He is molding and shaping you. With that thought in mind, prayerfully review the following questions. Answer the one which brings the greatest glory to God concerning you. 1). Where has your faith journey taken you? Or 2). How has God held you through trying times?

4. If you had to describe or define your faith journey in one sentence, what would it say? Record it below.

5. Prayerfully read Romans 3:21-31.

Paul concludes Romans 3 by pointing out the only method by which God justifies man - through faith and faith alone. That has always been God's way of setting people right with Himself. In Romans 3:31, Paul asks and answers an important question. Is the law null and void because of faith? His answer confirms that faith establishes the law rather than abolishing it. Jesus has fulfilled, accomplished, and satisfied every aspect of God's law. By the way, this is something that man could never achieve.

Faith is the essential component of God's divine plan. God never intended that we earn our righteousness. He knew it would be humanly impossible. The human condition called sin would have tainted your best efforts on your better days. Mercifully, that's what the law does - reveals sin.

To sum it up, faith confirms and supports the law in the sense that faith in Jesus fulfills all the obligations of the law. Therefore, don't fret! Everything required by the law has been satisfied through your faith in Christ Jesus. It's always been by faith, alone, in Christ alone! Complete Paul's summary statement below, beginning with the last phrase of Romans 3:29.

"Yes, of the Gentiles also, since *there is* one _____ who will _____ the circumcised _____ faith and the uncircumcised _____ faith. Do we then make _____ the law through faith? Certainly not! On the contrary, we _____ _____ _____" (Romans 3:29-31).

Lesson 11: A Review of Romans 1-7

Day Five: **Respond**

Romans' Theme Verse: "For I am not ashamed of the gospel of Christ, for it is the power of God to salvation for everyone who believes, for the Jew first and also for the Greek. For in it the righteousness of God is revealed from faith to faith; as it is written, 'The just shall live by faith' " (Romans 1:16-17).

You owe your thanks to God because you are justified by faith in Christ alone. That means you have Christ's righteousness by faith in Him. That's good news since you can't earn this justification (righteousness) through works or preserve and keep it through works, either. The grace and mercy of God have made it available only by believing in Him. So, as Abraham believed the promise, and it was counted to him as righteousness, you are his child as you come to saving faith by the same process. "Abraham believed in the Lord, and He accounted [credited, imputed] it to him for righteousness" (Genesis 15:6). Although thousands of years have passed, nothing has changed. Sin is still a transgression against God; faith is still faith; salvation is still salvation; and the gospel – the good news - that glorious promise of redemption to those who believe is always the same. The moment you believed, God credited your faith for righteousness as well. Although you might not look like it or feel righteous, it has been accomplished on your behalf because you believe. Rejoice, you are held by the mighty grip of God, and He will see you through. (See 1 John 2:25.) A faithful God has promised life in eternity with Him, and He can never lie!

As we conclude our review of Romans 1-7, let's review the weekly memory verses from Lessons 6-10. Although this is a simple exercise, God's Word is not. Working through these passages will encourage your faith and give you a better perspective of the Romans' journey thus far.

Pay close attention. These verses paint a beautiful portrait of God's love for not only you but for the **world**. Remember, "For God so loved the **world** that He gave His only begotten Son, that whoever believes in Him should not perish but have everlasting life. For God did not send His Son into the **world** to condemn the **world**, but that the **world** through Him might be saved" (John 3:16-17) [Emphasis added.] Take note, God is an impartial God and will save all who believe - all who call upon the name – Jesus. (See Romans 10:13 and Acts 2:21.)

These memory verses highlight the believer's spiritual journey to righteousness. When you believed, you obtained "right standing" before a Holy God through Jesus. His righteousness became your righteousness the instant you believed. One day soon, you will not only be with Jesus, but you will be like Him too! Remember this. A merciful God of unfailing love thought of you. He loves you completely, and made plans to have you with Him forever! ♥

Read and review each memory verse and answer the accompanying questions. Note: Your answers will come from each verse.

Lesson 6:

"Therefore, having been justified by faith, we have peace with God through our Lord Jesus Christ" (Romans 5:1).

1. How were you justified? _____ _____

2. In the process, you received something through our Lord Jesus Christ. What was it? Be specific.

Lesson 7:

"Therefore we were buried with Him through baptism into death, that just as Christ was raised from the dead by the glory of the Father, even so we also should walk in newness of life" (Romans 6:4).

3. You were buried into Jesus' death through something. What was it?

4. You should walk in newness of life. How did this occur?

Lesson 8:

"For the wages of sin is death, but the gift of God is eternal life in Christ Jesus our Lord" (Romans 6:23).

5. You earn something dreadful through sin. What is it?

6. On the contrary, God's gift is different. What is it, and through whom is it received?

Lesson 9:

"Therefore, my brethren, you also have become dead to the law through the body of Christ, that you may be married to another—to Him who was raised from the dead, that we should bear fruit to God" (Romans 7:4).

7. You are dead. How so?

8. You are married to another, to whom? _____
_____

9. Being raised from the dead you should do something unique. What is it?

10. In your own words, what is fruit to God?

Lesson 10:

"O wretched man that I am! Who will deliver me from this body of death? I thank God—through Jesus Christ our Lord!" (Romans 7:24-25).

11. In the first sentence of the verse, Paul's confession is bold. What is it and what does that mean?

12. Like Paul, all believers need deliverance. From what? _____ _____ _____

13. Paul is thankful! How are believers delivered, including you? Record the words from the passage.

You are invited to close in prayer. As you do, think about the goodness of God. Salvation is a Trinitarian plan from eternity past. Our merciful God knew you could never be righteous enough on your own. Even though Adam and Eve saw God, knew God, and fellowshipped with Him in the garden, they couldn't do it either.

Consequently, sin entered through the first Adam, and Jesus, the second Adam, settled the score on Calvary. There, Jesus conquered sin and death and celebrated victory over the grave. Rejoice, He has accomplished everything necessary to satisfy God's wrath against sin, not only for the world but concerning you. Therefore, as you pray, make it personal. Your God has indeed done great things for you!

Words of Jesus
"But Jesus answered them, saying, 'The hour has come that the Son of Man should be glorified. Most assuredly, I say to you, unless a grain of wheat falls into the ground and dies, it remains alone; but if it dies, it produces much grain' " (John 12:23-24).

Lesson 12: Life Through The Power Of The Holy Spirit
Romans 8:1-17

Day One: **Read**. Prayerfully Read Romans 8:1-17

Memory Verse: "There is therefore now no condemnation to those who are in Christ Jesus, who do not walk according to the flesh, but according to the Spirit" (Romans 8:1).

Romans 7:15-25 revealed your struggle with sin and the inadequacy of the law to make your flesh righteous. Although you did not become righteous by the law, you acknowledged that it succeeded in its purpose to reveal your sin. In Romans 8:1-17, Paul spotlights the Holy Spirit's work in believers through the law to make us righteous. That occurs as the law of God engages with the Spirit to sanctify us and conform us to the image of Christ Jesus. The ultimate goal of all believers is to be like Jesus and to one day be with Him in eternity. Simply stated, our desire should be to look like Jesus, love like Jesus, and live for Jesus. Some older theologians concluded this. The chief end of man is "to glorify God (see Romans 11:36 and 1 Corinthians 10:31) and to enjoy him forever" (Psalms 73:25–28).[2] To reinforce that concept of glorifying God, pastor, author, and theologian John Piper has said. "God is most glorified in us when we are most satisfied in Him." How beautiful; that's always a win-win! When we find our satisfaction in God, ultimately, He is glorified!

Therefore, the Law of God has accomplished its end. God's Law, ignited by His Spirit, opens our eyes to sin, seals God's truth in our hearts, and little by little brings God's Word to performance in our lives. That's our sanctification. The Holy Spirit uses the Law of God to make us aware of sin, prompts us to confess sin without fear, and repent or turn from it.

Additionally, the Spirit takes the Word and reveals God's perfect love and will for our lives. Through His Spirit, which resides in us, we grow in His grace through the knowledge of His truth. Then, as we yield in obedience to God's Word, we are **sanctified by the truth**. As the truth becomes a part of our lives (and is revealed in and through us), we partner with God to go about the Father's business! Just like Jesus. Jesus prayed that His Word would sanctify us. "For this sake I sanctify Myself, that they also may be sanctified in truth" (John 17:19).

---

[2] *The Westminster shorter catechism: with Scripture proofs*. (1996). (3rd edition.). Oak Harbor, WA: Logos Research Systems, Inc.

What's our part in it? Agreeing with God (His Word) and yielding to His Spirit's work in our lives. That's essentially doing what the Bible tells us, by faith and trusting the results to God. At its core, that what being sanctified in the truth means.

The sanctification process takes time. For most of us, a lifetime. That work will not be complete until we stand before Jesus, but the good news is this. The process rests entirely on God, and He has promised to see you through! He will never leave you as He found you because He loves you too much for that. Take note. All of God's promises have the total weight and authority of righteousness behind it. God can never lie! His Word will prevail and have its perfect way. Paul's confidence rested in God. He declared to the Philippians, "being confident of this very thing, that He who began a good work in you will complete it until the day of Jesus Christ" (Philippians 1:6) (Emphasis added.)

1. Through the blood of Christ, we are forgiven, although we see in Romans 8:1 that condemnation belonged to those who are "in Adam." Lest we forget, that would be all of humanity, including you, before salvation. You may recall, Paul instructed us concerning humanity's unrighteous condition numerous times in part one of our studies. He assured us that we were all conceived and born into sin; it's our gift or inheritance from Adam. For review, prayerfully read Psalm 51:5 and Romans 5:12. Next, read and record the first phrase of Romans 8:1 below.

2. For a stark contrast, read and review Romans 5:16 and 5:18. What was promised to those who are "in Christ?" Record Romans 5:18 below.

3. To describe the "walk" of those In Christ, complete Romans 8:1 below.

"There is therefore now no condemnation to those who are in Christ Jesus, who do not _____ according to the _____, but according to the _____" (Romans 8:1).

4. From Romans 8:2, the law of the Spirit of life in Christ Jesus made believers free. From what law were they freed? As you record your answer, make it personal. Rejoice, you are FREE.

The law of _____ and _____.

5. Thinking biblically, what does it mean to be free from the law of sin and death? What does it mean to you personally?

6. Read Romans 8:3. Using the appropriate phrase(s) from the verse, answer the following:

   a. Who took care of condemning sin in Christ for us?

   b. Why was the law unable to take care of condemning sin?

   c. How did God accomplish the work that condemned sin in the flesh? Be specific. Record the words of the verse in your answer.

7. Romans 8:3 says God's Son was "in the likeness of sinful flesh." Does this mean that Jesus was sinful? If possible, explain your answer by recording a verse of scripture the identifies Jesus' relationship to sin.

8. In Romans 8:4, what was fulfilled in those who do not "walk" according to the flesh but according to the Spirit? Be specific. Record the words of the verse in your answer.

9. Prayerfully read Romans 8:5. What is written about those who live in the flesh? About those who live in the spirit?

    flesh:

    spirit:

10. Read Romans 8:6. Your thought-life matters because it affects your life. How so? Our mind's inclinations guide us. They govern our actions, words, and deeds. In other words, your mind continually births or delivers a by-product and a result. Complete the thoughts below.

    a. Being carnally-minded is:

b. Thinking biblically, what does that mean spiritually and naturally?

c. Being spiritually minded is:

d. Thinking biblically, what does that mean spiritually and naturally?

Lesson 12: Life Through The Power Of The Holy Spirit
Romans 8:1-17

Day Two: **Research**. Review Romans 8:1-17

Memory Verse: "There is therefore now no condemnation to those who are in Christ Jesus, who do not walk according to the flesh, but according to the Spirit" (Romans 8:1).

I. Using a bible, bible dictionary, or concordance define the following **key words.**

peace v. 6

enmity v. 7

adoption v.15

heirs v.17

II. Read the following **key phrases.**

Spirit who dwells in you v. 11 - *spirit (pneuma)* - literally the *indwelling Christ* in you. You have His presence. The Holy Spirit resides in all believers. At the time of salvation, believers are sealed with the Holy Spirit as a guarantee of life. Therefore, *dwells, indwelling* refers to "how" Christ makes His home in you. The Spirit of Christ is "at home" in all believers. That's everyone who has put their faith, hope, and trust in Christ alone for forgiveness, salvation, and eternal life. Because Christ is in us, we are empowered to *"walk in the Spirit."* One Bible scholar said it like this. "God cannot condemn us, for the Holy Spirit enables the believer to *"walk in the Spirit,"* and thereby, meet His holy demands."

According to the *Pocket Lexicon to the Greek New Testament, "the Spirit is spiritual."* That makes perfect sense. The "Spirit" generally references the higher nature of man and his connection to and influence from the divine – that would be God. In essence, believers have a divine connection residing within. We enjoy breath and life through Christ's indwelling Spirit, but it's much more than that. The reality is, **we have life in God.** That identifies the inner being, which is God, from God, knows God, and can respond to God.

Review Romans 8:1-2; also read Romans 5:5 and Romans 8:9. Complete Romans 5:5 below.

"Now _____ does not disappoint, because the _____ of God has been poured out in our _____ by the Holy Spirit who was _____ _____ _____" (Romans 5:5).

Spirit of adoption v. 15 - *From the New American Standard Hebrew-Aramaic and Greek dictionaries: updated edition, we find that "adoption is a compound word coming from two root words, **huios** meaning 'a son,' and **tithēmi** meaning 'to place, lay, set — appointed.' The Greek compound word for adoption is **huiothesia**, which means to 'place as a son.'"*

Only Paul uses this Greek word for spiritual adoption in the New Testament. He references our spiritual adoption in his letters to the Romans, Galatians, and Ephesians. Paul makes it clear that our adoption is through God's gracious choice. Further, our adoption was predetermined before the foundation of the world. In other words, God predestined, predetermined, or foreknew everyone who would be adopted as sons and daughters through Jesus Christ. God not only knew those who would come to saving faith (in Christ alone), but He also called them to this faith.

This spiritual adoption is not the result of anything that we have earned. It is solely the outworking of God's love for sinners saved by grace. At its core, spiritual adoption embodies God's work of salvation. Its abundant benefits are linked to the believer's past and present as well as their future. Although we may not think about it in these terms, these benefits have an eschatological benefit because everyone will spend eternity somewhere. These spiritual benefits guarantee that one day, we will reign and rule with Jesus. And, if that weren't enough, through spiritual adoption, we become co-heirs with Christ and recipients of a rich spiritual inheritance.

With all of creation, we await deliverance from these bodies of flesh and the corrupt world in which we live. We owe our thanks to God. Our spiritual adoption guarantees and ensures that we will not only be with Him in eternity, but we will be like Him too. At long last, what we're longing for will be accomplished.

Prayerfully read Ephesians 1:4-14. These verses eloquently address all the spiritual blessings we have in Christ as children of God. Read the following verses from Ephesians 1:4-14 and circle the words which, in your opinion, reference our <u>abundant spiritual blessings</u> in Him.

"...just as He chose us in Him before the foundation of the world, that we should be holy and without blame before Him in love, 5 having predestined us to adoption as sons [and daughters] by Jesus Christ to Himself, according to the good pleasure of His will, 6 to the praise of the glory of His grace, by which He made us accepted in the Beloved.

7 In Him we have redemption through His blood, the forgiveness of sins, according to the riches of His grace 8 which He made to abound toward us in all wisdom and prudence, 9 having made known to us the mystery of His will, according to His good pleasure which He purposed in Himself, 10 that in the dispensation of the fullness of the times He might gather together in one all things in Christ, both which are in heaven and which are on earth—in Him. 11 In Him also we have obtained an inheritance, being predestined according to the purpose of Him who works all things according to the counsel of His will, 12 that we who first trusted in Christ should be to the praise of His glory.

13 In Him you also trusted, after you heard the word of truth, the gospel of your salvation; in whom also, having believed, you were sealed with the Holy Spirit of promise, 14 who is the guarantee of our inheritance until the redemption of the purchased possession, to the praise of His glory..." (Ephesians 1:4-14)

spirit of bondage...to fear v. 15 - From the *Greek-English Lexicon of the New Testament, a spirit of bondage is "a state or condition of subservience—slavery."* At the core of spiritual bondage, we discover that **"self,"**

1). desires to live after the flesh, or

2). lives under the law enduring its bondage of legalism and religious tradition.

Tragically, neither has known the liberty of grace. Instead, they're trapped. They're trapped in fear and self-righteous works rather than the love and acceptance of sonship and abandonment to God. As a believer, you must remember that you are hidden with Christ in God, and Christ's Spirit is "at home" with you. At the moment of salvation, Christ took up permanent residence in you. Subsequently, you're no longer a slave to fear, bound by fear, or controlled by fear. What was the fear? Bible scholars agree it was most assuredly death. Fear of death has plagued men's hearts forever. The author of Hebrews confirms that thought.

"Inasmuch then as the children have partaken of flesh and blood, He Himself likewise shared in the same, that through death He might destroy him who had the power of death, that is, the devil, and release those who through _____ of _____ were all their lifetime subject to _____" (Hebrews 2:14-15).

heirs of God; joint-heirs with Christ v. 17 - Believers are the legal recipients of God's estate and co-heirs with Christ. In other words, because we have been baptized into Christ, scripture assures us we share in His son-ship as well as His inheritance. Jesus will receive His inheritance by divine right, and we receive ours by divine grace through adoption. Presently, that status is confirmed as we share in His sufferings. One Bible scholar noted, "If one side of the cross involves Jesus taking believers' sin, the other side involves them sharing in His sufferings for righteousness." All believers know the cost of discipleship. We have experienced the same hatred that Jesus suffered and promised us because we are baptized into Christ. One day we will also share His resurrection glory through our coming resurrection. Because we are sons and daughters of the Most High God and co-heirs with Christ Jesus, we will share with Jesus all that our heavenly Father has to give.

An heir of God

According to Galatians 3:29, what awaits those in Christ and why?

Our inheritance will be more than we could ever hope or imagine. Paul was given a glimpse of what lies ahead. He was transported or "caught up" to the third heaven - Paradise - the abode of God. In God's presence, Paul saw with his eyes and heard with his ears, "inexpressible words." (See 2 Corinthians 12:4.) Although we know Paul is not short on words, he could not articulate all he saw and heard because he was not permitted to share these things in scripture. Nevertheless, our inheritance is secure. Scripture provides us a glimpse that includes eternal salvation, God Himself, His glory, the resurrection of our bodies, and everything in the universe.

In summary, let's take a quick look at a portion of our inheritance.

Eternal salvation

Read Titus 3:7. Through our Savior, something of eternal significance has occurred. What happened by His grace, and what have you become? Be specific.

Read John 3:16. What is promised and why?

God Himself

Read Lamentations 3:24. What are your portion and hope?

Read and record the promise of Revelation 21:3 below.

His glory

Read Romans 5:2. Through Jesus, you have access by faith into something which causes you and all believers to rejoice. What do believers access by faith, and in what do we rejoice?

Our bodily resurrection

Read 1 Thessalonians 4:15-17. Whether you are alive or dead when Christ returns, several things will occur. First, what will happen to the living and the dead at the coming of the Lord?

Everything in the universe

Read Hebrews 1:2. Everything that exists will ultimately come under the control of the Son of God, the Messiah. 1). Who has appointed heir of all things, and 2). Through whom were the worlds made?

Lesson 12: Life Through The Power Of The Holy Spirit
Romans 8:1-17

Day Three: **Receive**. Review Romans 8:1-17

Memory Verse: "There is therefore now no condemnation to those who are in Christ Jesus, who do not walk according to the flesh, but according to the Spirit" (Romans 8:1).

1. Read and review Romans 8:7-8 and answer questions 1 – 3

    a. Why is the carnal mind not subject to the law of God?

    b. Can the carnal mind ever be subject to the law of God? Yes or no?

    c. What is impossible for those in the flesh?

2. Read and record Romans 8:8 below.

3. If you are not in the flesh, but the spirit, what dwells in you? Be specific.

4. Read Romans 8:9. Here we see a testimony that the Holy Spirit is "at home" in all believers. Bible scholars agree that this is the most explicit verse in scripture that pinpoints the moment of conversion in believers.

   a. Thinking biblically and reflecting upon your personal experience, when does this occur?

   b. What does Paul mean when he says, "if anyone does not have the Spirit of Christ…" Record the remainder of Romans 8:9 to respond.

   c. Thinking biblically, what is guaranteed when God's Spirit "takes up residence in you?"

5. Read and review Romans 8:10. What sure things occur "if" Christ is in you?

   a. To the body:_____

   b. To the spirit_____

6. Read and review Romans 8:11.

   a. According to the first phrase of Romans 8:11, which specific Spirit "dwells" in you?

   b. What will He give you? Be specific.

7. Romans 8:11 promises "life to your mortal body." Can you define this life in a sentence or two? What does it mean to you personally? To aid your response, read and review 1 John 4:13 and Colossians 1:27.

♥ Heart-Check For Today

8. Romans 8:10-11 speak of life and death. That's crucial because what we believe is a matter of life and death. We were all dead in our trespasses and sin, but thanks be to God, we are justified and obtain right standing before God because we have believed in Jesus for salvation and eternal life. What a beautiful word for believers. Only we have "life in the Spirit," know forgiveness and have fellowship with God through Jesus Christ, our Lord. Right standing before God equals life, and the absence of God equals death. Do these verses prompt you to share with others about the abundant life that comes from faith in Christ alone? If so, pause now to pray for your unsaved friends and family members. Will you commit to pray for their salvation regularly? It is the author's belief you are saved today because someone has prayed for you. Consider this work closest to God's heart. When we pray for the souls of men, we partner with God in His work of salvation. You are invited to pray.

9. Read and review Romans 8:11.

a. In this passage, Paul draws a powerful conclusion about something Christ gives believers. What is it?

b. The same Spirit that raised Christ from the dead has taken up residence in you. How astounding! Although your mortal body will one day perish, the Spirit of God will raise your body from the dead. Sweet sisters, because you believe you have life, and your spirit is alive and testifies with God's Spirit that you have life in Him. (See Romans 8:16.) Therefore, you can enjoy the peace and confidence of knowing you are justified in the sight of God. Meditate on that knowledge for a moment and, then, in the space provided, record the first word that comes to your mind.

10. We are alive through the Spirit. Paul connected the resurrection of Jesus to the resurrection of His followers. As a reoccurring theme, he wrote of our association with Christ's resurrection and life in the Spirit not only to the Romans (see Romans 8:11) but to the Corinthians and Thessalonians as well. Read the following verses. Since believers have *"hope in the resurrection,"* let's review these precious promises concerning God's resurrection power. Complete the verses below.

"And _____ both raised up the _____ and will also raise _____ _____ by His _____" (1 Corinthians 6:14).

"knowing that He who raised up the _____ _____ will also raise _____ up with _____, and will present _____ with you" (2 Corinthians 4:14).

"For if we _____ that Jesus died and _____ again, even so God will bring with _____ those who _____ in Jesus" (1 Thessalonians 4:14).

11. Read and review Romans 8:11 again. There is a qualifier associated with our resurrection. What is it?

Lesson 12: Life Through The Power Of The Holy Spirit
Romans 8:1-17

Day Four: **Reflect**. Prayerfully Review Romans 8:1-17

Memory verse: "There is therefore now no condemnation to those who are in Christ Jesus, who do not walk according to the flesh, but according to the Spirit" (Romans 8:1).

Now we come to the **power of the resurrection**. In Philippians 3:10, Paul wrote of the *"power of His [Christ's] resurrection."* Paul desired to know Jesus and the power of His resurrection. Did you catch that? More than anything else, Paul wanted a heightened knowledge of Jesus and deeper intimacy with Him. He wanted to live in the resurrection power. What does that mean? It means walking in the same power, energy, and strength that raised Jesus from the dead. The word for power in Greek is **dunamai,** which means *"to be able; to be capable of."* At the root of its meaning, we find the emphasis rests on the ability, capability, and strength of performance. That is where we get the word dynamite; this power is explosive and has God's strength and force behind it. You possess the same resurrection power, and it's always available - at the ready - since the same Spirit, Christ's Spirit, resides in you. Remember, the moment you came to faith, God's Spirit took up residence in you, by His grace and for His glory.

1. In the life of believers, God's resurrection power is manifested in many ways. Examine the list below to discover the empowering strength of the resurrection which lives in you. For reflection, are these powers present in you?

_____Power over temptation and sin   _____Power to "fear not"
_____Power to choose joy   _____Power to die to self
_____Power to grow in faith   _____Power to serve
_____Power to rise above your circumstances _____Power to pray
_____Power to love all others   _____Power to seek the will of God
_____Power to forgive everyone   _____Power to do the will of God
_____Power to be His witness   _____Power to endure trials and persecution
     (Note: this begins at home)

2. Are you embracing the resurrection power in you? Paul knew his life was impotent apart from Christ, and it is the same with us. He was weak but not powerless. Paul knew that <u>he had power</u> through the Spirit of Christ, which was "at home" in him. That's why he could count it all loss except the excellence of the knowledge of Christ...and the power of His resurrection. As you reflect on Romans 8:1-17, complete the passages from Philippians 3:8-11 below.

"Yet indeed I also count _____ things _____ for the _____ of the knowledge of Christ Jesus my _____, for whom I have _____ the loss of all _____, and count them as _____, that I may gain _____ and be found in _____, not having my own _____, which *is* from the _____, but that which *is* through _____ in Christ, the _____ which is from God by _____; that I may know _____ and the _____ _____ _____ _____, and the _____ of His _____, being conformed to His death, if, by any means, I may attain to the _____ from the dead" (Philippians 3:8-11).

3. Pray through the list in question 1 and consider these and other ways Christ's resurrection power manifests itself in you. Do you feel the resurrection power? How have you most recently enjoyed Christ's resurrection power at work in you?

4. Read and review Romans 8:12-17 and answer the following questions.

   a. Although we are debtors, what are we not in debt to? v. 12

   b. If we live according to the flesh, what happens? v. 13

c. To live by the Spirit, what must believers do? v. 13

d. How are we identified if we are "led by the Spirit of God?" v. 14

e. As believers, we did not receive a spirit of what? v. 15

f. What was that spirit linked to? v. 15

g. Instead, we received what Spirit? v. 15

h. This Spirit enabled us to what? Be specific. v. 15

i. v.16 The _____ Himself bears witness with our _____ that we are children of _____ v. 17 and if children, then _____ - heirs of _____ ..."

j. Prayerfully read and complete the conditional phrase of Romans 8:17 below.
"and joint heirs with Christ, if_____
_____."

Lesson 12: Life Through The Power Of The Holy Spirit
Romans 8:1-17

Day Five: **Respond**. Review Romans 8:1-17

Memory Verse: "There is therefore now no condemnation to those who are in Christ Jesus, who do not walk according to the flesh, but according to the Spirit" (Romans 8:1).

A relationship has been established through our spiritual adoption, and believers can cry "Abba Father." (See Romans 8:15.) Through this adoption, our legal standing is established as heirs of God, co-heirs with Christ. "Abba" is the Hebrew word for father or daddy. At the core of its meaning, the emphasis rests on intimacy and relationship. No one ever became a father apart from a relationship. This type of relationship is only possible through the natural birth or legal adoption of a child. "Abba" identifies your father, not your cousin's or best friend's father. Only your father is Abba. The Lord's prayer begins, "Our Father," which would read in Aramaic, "Our Abba." In the plural sense, these words unite all believers under the headship of one Father, who is God the Father, the Creator of all things - including us! He – Abba - is the preeminent lover of our souls.

Our Lord Jesus prayed "Abba" in the Garden of Gethsemane. Mark's gospel records:

"Then they came to a place which was named Gethsemane; and He said to His disciples, 'Sit here while I pray.' And He took Peter, James, and John with Him, and He began to be troubled and deeply distressed. Then He said to them, 'My soul is exceedingly sorrowful, even to death. Stay here and watch.' He went a little farther, and fell on the ground, and prayed that if it were possible, the hour might pass from Him. And He said, 'Abba, Father, all things are possible for You. Take this cup away from Me; nevertheless, not what I will, but what You will' " (Mark 14:32-36).

At the most heart-wrenching time in Jesus' earthly life and ministry, what did he pray? "Abba – Father" - My father. It was so passionate and tender, so personal and intimate. It's as if Jesus cried, "Daddy, it's me, Jesus! I need you!" To Jesus, His Daddy was much more than the Godhead of the Trinity and the Creator of all things; He was Daddy. He was not only His Heavenly Father - He was His personal Father – as well! There is history, intimacy, and relationship supporting these words. In His hour of greatest need, Jesus cried out to His Daddy – "Abba, Father."

The Greek-English Lexicon of the New Testament states concerning Abba – "a Greek transliteration of an Aramaic word meaning 'father'): (titles for God, literally 'father') one who combines aspects of supernatural authority and care for his people—'Father.'" In its Aramaic transliteration, the word Abba only occurs three times in the New Testament. Abba is found in Mark 14:36, Galatians 4:6, and Romans 8:15.

Earthly relationships can be challenging at times because they involve sinful people. As a result, all our relationships are tainted by sin and self. Because it's not heaven until heaven, even parental relationships can be difficult to navigate. Therefore, it is easy to understand how a bad relationship with an earthly father might distort our relationship with God, our Father.

Bad memories, judgment, criticism, sexual abuse, or violence could affect your relationship with God. When this occurs, we are in error. God is so "other than" your earthly Father. He created you with love and divine purpose - on purpose! (See Psalm 139.) He has good things planned for you. (See Jeremiah 29:11.) You are not being judged or criticized by your heavenly Father. He loves you to the max, even now. There is not one thing you could do to cause Him to love you more completely than He already does and already has. (See Romans 5:8.) His love for you is perfect, holy, and without end - it's complete! You are on His heart and mind. When Jesus died for you, you were the last thought on His mind. You were the prize, and His knowledge that you would be His eternally made it all worthwhile. His faithful love has always had eternity in view. Sweet sister, regardless of how you feel or what the enemy has told you, you are (and were) worth dying for! You are His child; He adores you, not as you should be, but just as you are. Rejoice! Your "Abba" delights in you and sings praises over you! (See Zephaniah 3:17.)

1. Regardless of the relationship you experienced with your earthly father, you have a good Heavenly Father. "God is good!" So, with a heart of thanks, record Psalm 136:1 below.

2. That awesome and powerful, perfect God is your heavenly Father. He is your "Abba." Do you think of Him this way? In your hour of need, do you cry out, "Abba Father?" Have you ever cried out "Abba Father?" Yes or no? _____

3. God is approachable. He waits attentively to hear from His children - including you. You are invited to share a testimony of an occasion when you cried, "Abba Father," in anguish or bitterness of soul. In your statement, please include how "Abba" responded in your hour of great need.

A Missionary Testimony.

Before our ministry relocation to Jerusalem, we enjoyed a three-month stay in Israel, serving various ministries and making preparations for our move. In the first month, we stayed in a modern hotel overlooking the walls of the Old City of Jerusalem. It was a beautiful, clean hotel with good food, modern conveniences, and a gorgeous swimming pool. One hot sunny day, we discovered a break in our busy schedule and decided to take advantage of the "down time" by relaxing at the pool. I planned to write and pray, so I packed a small bag, and off we went.

Shortly after settling in, I heard laughter and splashing at the other end of the pool. From the broken silence, I knew others had joined us. I glanced up from my writing and noticed a young father and son playing in the water. They were speaking Hebrew, and at the time, of course, I understood no Hebrew or Arabic. I was indeed an alien in a foreign land. As they played water games, they provided a whimsical backdrop of joyful chatter to buffet the sound of traffic from the street below. Over time, I noticed a repetitive rhythm to their conversation. The little boy would say "something..... Abba," and his father would respond with the same reply every time.

Although I had no idea what either of them was saying, I could recognize in each exchange that their words were always the same. Their water play and the rhythmic conversation continued for about forty-five minutes.

As their playtime ended, a noisy and tearful commotion ensued. I glanced up to see the child stumbling, crying, and speaking loudly as his tiny hands flailed wildly and groped thin air. In contrast, his father remained calm, never leaving his side. Leaning down, he spoke soft and tender words in Hebrew while guiding his son to safety. After a few seconds, the frantic child found his father's open arms and melted into them. Instantly, the tears subsided, and all fears seemed to melt away. His whole countenance changed. He had found safety and rest in the arms of his father. He was secure, and he knew it.

What I had imagined as a simple water game was not a game at all. The child was blind! He couldn't see, and that's why he called out repeatedly. He needed to hear his father's voice to know that he was safe. He needed to know that his father was there. He needed to be in the shelter of his father's arms. For this tiny Jewish boy, it was not a game at all. His father was everything – including his eyes. The father provided all he needed.

While in the water, the child had been crying out, "Abba, where are you?" And his father's reassuring reply, "I am here; you are safe." Immediately, I was flooded with tears and emotion. What a beautiful picture God had painted for me. My Abba had revealed to me through their aquatic banter how near He truly is. He is on my side. Forever! He is at the ready always; He is at my side!

Verses filled my mind, and I attempted to capture them as tears filled my eyes and spilled on the page. Then, God's Spirit sweetly whispered to me. "I will never leave you or forsake you... I am closer than a brother... All who are weary and heavy-laden... Come to me, and I will give you rest... Call upon the name of the Lord... Seek first the kingdom of God and His righteousness... I am your fortress and strength... God is love... I am the way, the truth, and the life... I will give you joy in the morning... He who began a good work in you will... I am from everlasting to everlasting... There is shelter under my wings... For God so loved... The Lord, the Lord God merciful..."

God's timing was perfect. Six thousand miles from home, in a foreign land, surrounded by strange and curious sights and sounds, God calmed my unspoken, unrealized anxieties. I was embarking on foreign missionary service that would remove me from all I had ever known, including my children. I realized that I might never see them or home again, yet it's as if God was saying, "Follow me, I've got this. I will guide you, comfort you, and give you strength. I will never leave your side. I am your Abba, Father!"

In my unspoken hour of need, God had guided us to the pool at the appointed time. He knew what I needed even before I did. God had pulled back the curtain to show me how near He truly is. His arms are always outstretched in love to receive. He beckoned my heart, "Cry out to me!" I will hold you; I will guide you; I am the lamp unto your feet. It's as if He said, "Let me be your eyes, I will guide you. You may stumble, but I've got you my sweet daughter. I will never leave you or forsake you."

I experienced an instant heart change that day as my missionary heart was fortified and strengthened. I stepped into a heightened intimacy with my Abba that very moment. He assured me that He is there for you and me. He will uphold each of us and love us into the Kingdom, literally. He will never leave us or forsake His children. He won't let go! He is a faithful God in the promise-keeping business. Rejoice! He's got you! He always had a plan to save you, and He will see you through. Your Abba Father is there for you!

4. Would you take the time to unburden your heart? Moving forward, will you take the time to cry, "Abba, Father," each day? He is there waiting with open arms for you.

5. Read Romans 8:15. What have you received?_____

Notice that Romans 8 ends the same way it begins. With no condemnation, none whatsoever. Instead, Romans 8 speaks of justification by grace through faith for those who have believed. Notice too; there are no qualifiers in Romans 8. Anyone, anywhere, throughout history, regardless of their past, is justified by grace through faith, and from that moment, there is **no condemnation**. How exciting! God is a God of inclusivity. Faith is no respecter of people; all people are included, and none are condemned. The rich, poor, old, young, black, white, brown, etc., we are all the same. Because we have His Spirit, we can all bear fruit to God. Theologians refer to Romans 8 as the "no condemnation" book of scripture. One pastor and theologian noted, "The Holy Spirit dominates the entire chapter, for it is through the indwelling Spirit that we overcome the flesh and live a fruitful Christian life."

In Romans 8, we discover that since the Spirit of Christ is "at home" in us, there is no condemnation, no obligation to the law, and no separation from God through Jesus Christ, our Lord. Please note. We are not condemned, we are not under obligation, and we are never separated from the love and fellowship of God. He has done it all. We see from our memory verse, **"There is therefore now no condemnation to those who are in Christ Jesus, who do not walk according**

to the flesh, but according to the Spirit" (Romans 8:1). You can rejoice because there is no sin, past, present, or future that can be held against you. What marvelous news! Jesus paid all the penalty, and His very righteousness is imputed to you because you have believed! That's a divine legal decision, and no one and no sin can ever reverse His will. Nor can anything separate you from the love of God. (For clarity, you may want to review Romans 8:31-39.) You are the daughter of the Highest God and King, and His lavish love for you is without end!

6. Let's end in prayer. Would you close your eyes like the small child in Jerusalem and whisper, "Abba, Father?" Now, imagine His strong arms around you, a breath away, holding you and guiding you. Hear His tender whisper to your heart... **"I love you, I will never leave you or forsake you** (write your name here) _____**, I am on your side and at your side, My beloved daughter, I am here for you!"** Let's put down a stone of remembrance today. You are invited to record the date of time of your prayer below. Sometime in the future, you will be encouraged by your growth and heightened intimacy with your "Abba, Father" from this day forward. **Date and time of prayer:** _____

Words of Jesus
"Then He said to her, 'Your sins are forgiven' " (Luke 7:48).

Lesson 13: Future Glory and More Than Conquerors
Romans 8:18-39

Day One: **Read**. Prayerfully Read Romans 8:18-39

Memory Verse: "For I am persuaded that neither death nor life, nor angels nor principalities nor powers, nor things present nor things to come, nor height nor depth, nor any other created thing, shall be able to separate us from the love of God which is in Christ Jesus our Lord" (Romans 8:38-39).

Review Romans 8:18-19 and answer the following questions.

1. We see from Romans 8:18 that although believers suffer presently, something will soon be revealed. What will be revealed in and through us soon?

2. From Romans 8:19, what eagerly awaits for the revealing of the sons of God?

3. Review Romans 8:20-21 and answer the following questions.

    a. From Romans 8:20, to what was creation unwillingly subjected?

    b. Also, from verse 20, who subjected it in hope? Be specific.

c. Prayerfully review Romans 8:21. One day soon, from what will creation be delivered?

d. According to verse 21, creation will be "*delivered into*" something as well. Into what?

4. Review Romans 8:22. The whole of creation _____ and _____ with what until now?

5. According to Romans 8:23, we groan within ourselves even though we have what?

6. Also, from v. 23, what do we eagerly await? Be specific.

7. Thinking biblically, what are the first fruits of the Spirit?

8. Read Romans 8:24. We are saved into hope, but apparently, hope is not hope after all. Why? Because hope that is seen is not hope; it never is. We do, however, wait for what we cannot see. Read and record Romans 8:25 below.

9. For review, what carries us through our times of suffering? Review Romans 8:24-25 for your response.

10. Having been saved and justified, we are waiting on something specific. What is it? For clarity, review what Paul told Timothy in Titus 3:7. Record your answer below.

11. Read and review Romans 8:26 and answer the following:

   a. Who helps us in our weaknesses?

   b. We need this help to accomplish what? _____

c. "but the _____ Himself makes _____ for us with _____ which cannot be uttered" (Romans 8:26).

12. Read and review Romans 8:27 and answer the following:

   d. What does He search?

   e. What specifically does He know?

   f. He makes what for the saints?

   g. Complete Romans 8:27 below. All this is accomplished "...according to the _____ ____ _____."

Understanding Our Weaknesses

Upon examination of Romans 8:26, we realize that although the Spirit always prays in the will of God, we have found ourselves unable to pray as we ought. Quite frankly, sometimes, the words simply don't come. One scholar noted that *"our weaknesses"* are rooted in our lack of understanding regarding prayer.

That is not a new problem. Prayer has always been a great mystery of spiritual life. We find that a two-fold problem fuels this great mystery. First, the significance of prayer is misunderstood, and second, we neglect or avoid prayer even though it's the believer's greatest tool. Subsequently, we either don't pray effectively or skip prayer altogether. Many believers would say this is their greatest challenge and hardest ministry of all. After faithful Bible study, failure in prayer tops the list.

Even though the disciples knew that prayer was crucial, they, too, lacked understanding. But here's what they did know. Daily, they saw Jesus retreat to prayer. They knew that somehow Jesus was strengthened and supported through prayer. They also knew that prayer was Jesus' first ministry. Sure, His mission was people, but they understood His power and purpose were realized through prayer. Lastly, they knew that Jesus was always about His Father's business; He told them so; and, then, lived that out. Therefore, they knew there was a spiritual connection. It's important to note that Jesus was on God's mission, not His own. Jesus described His earthly mission as follows. "For I have come down from heaven, not to do My own will, but the will of Him who sent Me" (John 6:38). Look at that verse and consider this question. How could Jesus know the next step or His Father's plan if He neglected prayer? So, although prayer seemed daunting, the disciples understood that they had to master this mysterious spiritual discipline called prayer. Ultimately, they faced their profound weakness and implored Jesus to teach them to pray!

It is the same with us. If you want to be "on a mission" with God, prayer is your launching pad, too! It's where believers engage with a loving Father and yield their lives to put the gospel truth into action. Because prayer connects believers to God, it is powerful and holy. Prayer is the vehicle by which believers (1) enter into God's presence; (2) receive their marching orders; and (3) partner with God.

So, how do we partner with God through prayer? It's relatively simple. At its core, it means agreeing with God (His Word) and doing God's work, God's way. It requires yielding to Him, loving Him, and loving and serving people while expecting nothing in return. Mostly, it comes down to keeping the greatest commandments. According to Jesus, our answer appears in Mark 12. What did Jesus say about the greatest commandments? He instructed the scribes by saying, "The first of all the commandments *is:* 'Hear, O Israel, the Lord our God, the Lord is one. And you shall love the Lord your God with all your heart, with all your soul, with all your mind, and with all your strength.' This *is* the first commandment. And the second, like *it, is* this: 'You shall love your neighbor as yourself.' There is no other commandment greater than these" (Mark 12:29-31).

Look closely at Jesus' Words from verses 30 and 31, focusing on the word "*love.*" In these phrases, Jesus transforms *"love"* (a noun) into a verb, where a verbal response is required. It occurs as love springs to life. In so doing, it becomes more than a mere utterance. Love now has life (energy) and becomes a sincere and intense, heartfelt expression or emotion that moves after a pattern and type of God. *That love* is supported or undergirded by an accompanying beneficial response, and guess what? From the original language, that "love" is a command. Who does that "love" benefit? Others, of course, and ultimately God's Kingdom. That love - that God-inspired love - fills the heart to overflowing. How ideal! Here's how that love operates.

Since sacrificial love flows from God, it engages with Him and responds to Him. Therefore, it can't help but explode and move forward with good works of genuine affection. Just as God planned, we pray and fill up with Him, and love moves and advances toward the greater need. Like a heat-seeking missile, this love seeks to serve as its Creator wills. That love is not only from God and engaged with God, but it's also in tune with God. It does God's work, God's way! Not to oversimplify, but God's love has always responded to humanity's greatest need, and it's never in short supply. Prayer will ignite life-giving "love" every time. Incidentally, that's why God sent us Jesus! We needed a Savior! Believing in Jesus was, is, and will always be humanity's most urgent need.

So as you can see, these commandments necessitate loving God and others above yourself. That involves prayer, patience, and putting all others first. And not just in word only - but as outlined above - in action and deed. Remember, what we do supports what we confess and believe, and it's all to the honor and glory of God.

Lastly, faithful, heartfelt prayer not only positions us to yield our lives to Him, but it provides us a platform from which to praise and worship Him. After all, He alone is worthy of all honor and praise. So, perhaps prayer embodies more than you knew. Although you are invited to lay your petitions before God, it's best to remember that He is not a genie in a bottle. Albeit true, He delights in blessing us, but we must understand that His work and grace extend far beyond us. Prayer is crucial, but it takes time, and Jesus knew this. But guess what? Jesus was far busier than you'll ever be, but He did not neglect His time in prayer.

Make It Personal

As you bring today's lesson to a close, take a few minutes to think about your prayer life. How are you doing in that area of faithfulness? Remember, prayer is the greatest weapon we have as believers. I've said before, "There is no one stronger than a 90-pound woman as she arises from prayer." Once she has met with Jesus, she's encouraged to do God's work, God's way, because, in His presence, she's reassured and empowered; she's equipped and made ready. In His presence, all her insecurities and doubts flee because the enemy's schemes cannot prevail in the presence of a Holy God. Through prayer, she's infused with courage and undergirded with strength. Then, she's prepared to love others, choose joy, and face life's trials and temptations, whatever they may be. Now, she can love and serve all others because God so loves her. This author believes prayer changes everything because it does, namely us!

Pause now, and be honest with yourself. Are you faithful in prayer? If not, start by praying that God gives you a devoted prayer life and a prayer language as well! He will do it and much more than you might ever hope or imagine. God delights in you and plans to use you in prayer. When you feel prompted to pray, do so immediately, and God will richly reward your faithfulness. He will fill you with love, direction, hope, joy, peace, patience, etc.

When prayer becomes your first line of defense, instead of your last resort, you not only look more like Christ, but your confident poise conveys that you are His. Praying first assures everyone that your hope rests not in yourself or them but Jesus. As you cultivate a lifestyle of prayer, those around you will know that your hope rests wholly in God!

Pledge To Pray

Take a few minutes to close in prayer. Ask Jesus to burden you to pray. He will do just that! He delights to answer this question every time. You're invited to make a personal pledge of commitment now by saying, "I am committed to praying and leaving the results to God." Lay up a stone of remembrance today by recording the date and time of your pledge below.

    Date: Time:

One final word concerning prayer. Some of us will struggle to pray because we are distracted.

You can, however, be more successful than you might think. If you desire accountability in this area, ask for it. Find a friend to partner with in prayer. It's not only a marvelous thing to do, but it's biblical. Share your prayer requests with them as well as your praise reports and victories. They will be encouraged too. Ideally, you can promote one another's faithfulness in prayer.

Lastly, get a pray journal and track your progress. Over time, you will see that a faithful God delights to answer your prayers! When hard times come, a prayer journal full of victories is a handy weapon for your spiritual toolbox! Enjoy the journey!

Lesson 13: Future Glory and More Than Conquerors
Romans 8:18-39

Day Two: **Research**. Prayerfully Review Romans 8:18-39

Memory Verse: "For I am persuaded that neither death nor life, nor angels nor principalities nor powers, nor things present nor things to come, nor height nor depth, nor any other created thing, shall be able to separate us from the love of God which is in Christ Jesus our Lord" (Romans 8:38-39).

I. Using a bible, bible dictionary, or concordance define the following **key words.**

glory v. 18

futility v. 20

perseverance v. 25

intercession v. 27

predestined v. 30

II. Read the following **key phrases.**

bondage of corruption v. 21- All of creation is bound and enslaved to decay. From the *Greek-English Lexicon of the New Testament*, "...to rot or decay, in reference to organic matter—'to rot, to decay, decay.' Regarding v. 21, the creation itself will be set free from the slavery to decay' or '... the inevitable tendency to decay.' " As you can see from Romans 8:21, Paul personifies nature. From the Garden of Eden, all creation is longing for transformation, for deliverance, and freedom from the curse and its effects. Let's go back to the Garden for a review.

Read Genesis 3:17. Who was God speaking to, what was the specific curse, and for whose sake?

Read Genesis 5:29. What did Lamech say concerning Noah? Record the verse below.

first fruits of the Spirit v. 23 - Metaphorically speaking, just as the first apple on a tree provides hope in the coming harvest, we, too, have "fruitful" evidence of our future harvest or transformation into the likeness of Christ Jesus. All believers have a witness or testimony of His "indwelling Spirit," which is "at home" with us. According to Paul, that is the "first-fruit" of the Spirit, who sealed our hearts at salvation as a guarantee that a harvest is coming. These "first-fruits" are an eschatological (end times) pledge, guarantee, deposit - a down payment - of what awaits us as part of our future inheritance. All believers are waiting and groaning to be conformed to the image of Jesus. A fuzzy feeling or emotion does not realize this; instead, it's evidenced and revealed through the "fruit" of our lives.

Read Galatians 5:22-23 and list the fruits of the Spirit in the space provided. Then, complete the last phrase of verse 23.

"But the fruit of the spirit is

"Against such, there is no _____" (Galatians 5:23).

adoption v. 23 - the legal process by which we became children of God. The emphasis is placed on God's divine choice to adopt us. From the *Greek-English Lexicon of the New Testament* – *"...to formally and legally declare that someone who is not one's own child is henceforth to be treated and cared for as one's own child, including complete rights of inheritance."*

With that definition in mind, prayerfully read and review Romans 8:15. You have not received "something" instead of receiving "something better." What did you <u>not receive</u>? Instead, what <u>did you receive</u>?

You/We did not receive:

You/We did receive:

Read and review Ephesians 1:5. Paul said you were predestined for adoption by Jesus. According to what? Be specific.

redemption of our body v. 23 - Our entire body will be redeemed or released from bondage. That includes not only our mortal, flesh, or physical body, but also the "will or fallenness" which presently wars against our Spirit. In salvation, we have hope that our bodies will someday be free from the bondage of sin and decay. Read and complete Philippians 3:20-21 below.

"For our citizenship is in _____, from which we also eagerly _____ for the Savior, the Lord Jesus Christ, 21 who will _____ our lowly _____ that it may be _____ to His glorious body, according to the working by which He is _____ even to subdue all _____ to _____" (Philippians 3:20-21).

will of God v. 27 - We can only know the will of God through what God has recorded for us in scripture and revealed to us by the power of His Holy Spirit. The Spirit which indwells you is God the Spirit - the third member of the Godhead - also known as the Trinity. Three essential things must be noted about God's Spirit:

1). It knows God's heart and mind,
2). Is in unity with God's heart and mind (at all times), and
3). Responds according to God's perfect and pleasing will

The Spirit simultaneously accomplishes these things to bring about the divine purposes of God. Simply stated, the overarching goal of God is that we "*be conformed*" to the image or likeness of His Son, Jesus. Prayerfully review 1 Corinthians 2:11. Who, alone, knows the things of God? Record the last phrase of 1 Corinthians 2:11 as your answer.

God's elect v. 33 - Those God chose to *be conformed* to the image of His Son. With one word – *elect* - Paul sums up Romans 8:14-15. Some scholars believe Romans 8:33 is the climax of Paul's letter to the Romans. From the *Theological Dictionary of the New Testament*, "*In conclusion, then, the whole of the divine work, salvation, and new creation, from its pre-temporal origin to the final glorification, is summed up in the one term. Because the community consists of God's elect, there is no more accusation or condemnation, since, grounded thus, it cannot be separated from the love of God. As the elect, Christians must love one another. The aim of "election" is love. He who is loved by God can now love in truth.*" In summary, we look most like Jesus when we love God with all our heart, soul, mind, and strength and love our neighbor as ourselves.

Read and review Romans 8:14-15. How do we become "sons of God?" Be specific.

Please take note. The doctrine of election is woven throughout both testaments. One Bible scholar made this observation concerning election's root meaning from the original Greek. He concluded, *"At its [election's] core meaning, we find that God not only chose the elect by Himself but for Himself to the praise of His own glory!"* [Emphasis added.] Did you catch that? God's elect was chosen by Him - on purpose - and with divine purpose. God is in the business of salvation. Rejoice! He is still calling those He has chosen from eternity past to be conformed to the image of His Son, by His grace, and for His ultimate glory.

It must be noted, however, that our election or predestination does not exempt us from the responsibility of coming to faith, confessing Christ as Lord, and repenting of sin. Genuine faith, which bears fruit, must exist and thrive in the elect of God. Furthermore, it's only realized as we respond to God. Read and record the powerful red-letter words of Jesus from John 6:44 below. Pay special attention to the first phrase of the verse. Underline God's divine work in salvation from the passage.

John 6:44

Lesson 13: Future Glory and More Than Conquerors
Romans 8:18-39

Day Three: **Receive**. Review Romans 8:18-39

Memory Verse: "For I am persuaded that neither death nor life, nor angels nor principalities nor powers, nor things present nor things to come, nor height nor depth, nor any other created thing, shall be able to separate us from the love of God which is in Christ Jesus our Lord" (Romans 8:38-39).

1. Review Romans 8:28. What works together for good? Be specific.

2. What two qualifiers are found in Romans 8:28?

   a. to those who:_____

   b. to those who:_____

3. ♥ <u>Heart-Check For Today</u>

Thinking biblically, what is God's purpose? If possible, share a verse that supports your thoughts.

4. Read Romans 8:29-30 and complete the following.

v 29 "For whom He foreknew, He also predestined to _____

_____

that He might be _____"

v 30 "Moreover whom He predestined, these He also _____;

whom He called, these He also _____;

and whom He justified, these He also _____."

5. Although God loves all of His creation, those who love God are unique to Him; they are His children. He has extraordinary things in store for those who love Him and obey Him. Let's look at Romans 8:28-30 again.

v. 28 - These are *called according to His purpose;*

v. 29 - His purpose is to *conform them to the image of His Son; and*

v. 30 - The climax or pinnacle is *God bringing them to glory.*

As you review these verses, what is the "good" that God has purposed for those who love Him?

6. God's love is from everlasting to everlasting. It will never end and never fail. He has loved you with an everlasting love from before the foundation of the world! Paul asks a summary question in Romans 8:31. Record the verse below.

♥ Heart-Check For Today

7. Reread Romans 8:31. God is for you, He loves you, and He has good things planned for you! Even now, He is working all things together for good because you love Him and are called according to His purpose. In contrast, our earthly relationships are not always so heavenly. We touched on relationships in last week's lesson. They can be challenging because they are all tainted by sin and self. We will encounter people in this life that are irregular or difficult for us to love. Tragically, sometimes these differences escalate to the point of irreconcilable differences.

With that thought in mind, pause a minute to think of those who might be against you. Hold them in your heart for just a minute and ask yourself this question, "Are they [your enemies] any match for God? Has God not forgiven you all things? Are you not empowered by His Spirit to love and forgive because He has loved and forgiven you?" Will you release them to God and commit to pray for your enemies? After all, you are His image-bearer and purveyor of truth and love on the earth; and this is your only scriptural response. Complete Matthew 5:43-44 below.

"You have heard that it was said, '*You shall* _____ *your neighbor* and _____ your enemy.' But I say to you, love your _____, bless those who _____ you, do _____ to those who hate you, and _____ for those who spitefully use you and persecute you..." (Matthew 5:43-44).

8. Review v. 32. What did God not spare? For what purpose? Complete the verse below.

   He who did not spare

9. According to Romans 8:32, God "*delivered Him [Jesus] up for us all.*"

   a. Thinking biblically, what does that mean?

   b. Make it personal. What does it mean to you?

10. Read and review Romans 8:33 and answer the following questions. Be specific.

   a. What is the question?

   b. What is the answer?

11. Read and review Romans 8:34. Christ does not condemn you but makes something for you while at the right hand of God. What does He make for you? Be specific.

12. Read and review Romans 8:37. What are you "through Him who loved us"?

13. Read and review Romans 8:35-37. Who shall separate us from the love of God? Record Romans 8:38 - 39 as your answer.

v. 38

v. 39

14. Paul was persuaded that nothing could ever separate him from the love of God. From the *Greek-English Lexicon of the New Testament, persuaded* means "to come to believe the certainty of something on the basis of being convinced—'to be certain, to be sure, to be convinced.'"

   a. Are you persuaded that nothing can separate you from the love of God? Circle yes or no?

   b. If you are so persuaded, record a verse that confirms your answer.

   c. If you are not so persuaded, please share your doubts with your leader or pastor at your earliest convenience.

Lesson 13: Future Glory and More Than Conquerors
Romans 8:18-39

Day Four: **Reflect**. Prayerfully Review Romans 8:18-39

Memory Verse: "For I am persuaded that neither death nor life, nor angels nor principalities nor powers, nor things present nor things to come, nor height nor depth, nor any other created thing, shall be able to separate us from the love of God which is in Christ Jesus our Lord" (Romans 8:38).

Romans Road Map: Where are you on the journey? You are where God has determined - precisely. Not just you, all of God's creation moves, lives, and breathes at the will and command of God. We exist at the pleasure of God to fulfill the purposes of God. Do you recall God's primary purpose? Namely that we "be conformed" to the image of His Son through sanctification and that we glorify Him. Only He is due all honor, glory, and praise. He aims to have it, and He will extract it from His children.

Let's look at that again. You are where you are today, doing what you are doing by the divine providence of God. Simply stated, God - the Creator of all things - is leading and guiding your life. Yes, even the small stuff. Yes, even those difficult, sometimes complicated things. He holds the whole world in His loving hands; He's got it all. So when hard times come or tragedy strikes, it has not escaped God. Hardship did not accidentally slip through His hands and land on you. Nor was it an evil plot to "trouble or bother" your life. Nothing can touch a child of God that surprises Him. You are His child, and His plan concerning you has left nothing to chance. Take note. There are "no happenstances" in the life of a child of God.

Paul stated, "And we know that all things work together for good to those who love God, to those who are the called according to His purpose" (Romans 8:28). From that verse, who is working all these things together for good? _____ This tremendous task has certainly not been left to us. If so, we would surely fail. We are not capable within ourselves of **doing everything** in a way that **accords with His purpose**. Jesus did it, but He was God in the flesh. Our mortal bodies war Spirit against the flesh. For us, perfection apart from Christ is humanly impossible. Paul confessed in Romans 7:14 that even he was carnal. At every moment in time from eternity past, God is being God. He is sustaining and upholding all of creation to fulfill His divine purpose.

Paul knew and was fully persuaded that God was working all things together for good. He knew that God loved Him. So, too, Paul knew that his election or calling was according to God's purpose. Incidentally, the first call is always to be His! That's when God's electing love rested on you and called you to faith in Christ. You are His, and He loves you, but because we live in a fallen world, even believers are not exempt from pain and suffering. Troubles will come! As we noted before, it "ain't" heaven yet. We live in this fallen world, which we are merely passing through.

On that thought, Jesus told us there would be trouble in this life. Therefore, we must look at our present struggles in light of our coming glory. (See Romans 8:18.) We cannot share in His glory if we have not shared in His suffering. Before we dig in, let's frame today's lesson by considering God's loving hand in it all - the good, the bad, and the ugly. Biblically speaking, that's known as the "doctrine of the providence of God."

Paul also knew the providence of God. He believed and trusted God was guiding his steps and circumstances by His grace and for His glory. In other words, Paul knew that God always has His divine purpose in view. He does not change His mind. Unlike us, He is not flakey, forgetful, or sometimes scatter-brained. From the first breath of your life until the very last one - guess what? God is in control.

1. Questions like these often come to mind when the doctrine of the providence of God surfaces. Review these questions and circle your answer.

    a. Do you believe that God is in control of all things? Yes or no?
    b. Do you believe that even bad things have a purpose in God's plan? Yes or no?
    c. Do you believe that God is "truly" working all things together for good? Yes or no?

2. God's providence affects all of His creation at all times. As Dr. Wayne Grudem explains, " *We may define God's providence as follows: God is continually involved with all created things in such a way that he (1) keeps them existing and maintaining the properties with which he created them; (2) cooperates with created things in every action, directing their distinctive properties to cause them to act as they do; and (3) directs them to fulfill his purposes.*"[3]

---

[3] Grudem, W. A. (2004). *Systematic theology: an introduction to biblical doctrine* (p. 315). Leicester, England; Grand Rapids, MI: Inter-Varsity Press; Zondervan Pub. House.

Dr. Grudem has covered it all. In light of this definition, we can see that God created all things, is in all things, and is always and perpetually in control of all things. God is immanent. He is existing or operating within all He created. God didn't merely create it all and then turn His back. He is permanently pervading and sustaining the entire universe and all it includes to fulfill His divine purpose. Prayerfully review and complete the exercise below. Note God's divine providence in these passages. Through the process, may your faith be strengthened.

a. Romans 11:36. "For of Him and through Him and to Him are _____ _____, to whom be glory forever. Amen.
b. Colossians 1:16. "For by Him _____ _____ were created that are in heaven and that are on _____, visible and invisible, whether thrones or dominions or principalities or powers. _____ _____ were created _____ _____ and _____ _____."

We will examine our future glory tomorrow. Today's lesson invites you to reflect upon God's Word as you consider your *"present suffering"* in light of your *"future glory."*

In Romans 8:18-30, Paul moves us from this present life's struggle to our future glory. He jumps right in by referencing our coming resurrection. Paul boldly proclaims, "For I consider that the sufferings of this present time are not worthy to be compared with the glory which shall be revealed in us" (Romans 8:18).

The Romans not only heard Paul's message - they got it! They well-understood that for believers, the ultimate persecution or suffering could mean death - martyrdom. That end is not an overreach. The persecution of believers is not new; the practice is as old as time. Abel was martyred. How so? His brother, Cain, despised his offering of faith, which proved acceptable to God. The story unfolds in Genesis 4:1-16. (Note: Jesus referenced Abel as the first to be martyred in Matthew 23:35.)

Even today, more Christians are martyred for their faith than ever before. That may seem a bit excessive or extreme, but it's true. Christianity Today and The Christian Post both report that more than 100,000 Christians are martyred each year. In 2013, Time.com said the deaths of Christian martyrs doubled in Syria. That's shocking news since the report also revealed the number of those martyred had surpassed the worldwide total from 2012. That is not only shocking but telling indeed! We must remember that even though this news rattles us, God is in control. He is bringing all things to His desired end. Therefore, as things escalate around the world, we must anticipate His coming.

As believers, we know that our suffering, although intense, it's momentary. With that thought in mind, we must remember three important facts. First, God is in control; and second, our ultimate victory and glorification come with death. Third, life is our training ground. Our earthly time is short-lived relative to eternity. Lastly, we are spiritual beings having a human experience, not human beings having a spiritual experience. When this sinks in, we stand a better chance of looking more like Jesus and enduring our "momentary or present suffering" with grace. That grace, the steadfast grace through faith, glorifies God.

3. Although we don't look for suffering or invite it, it finds us. Jesus told the disciples that it was to be expected. He held it out as a sure prospect for all His disciples, us too. Just so you know, disciples are all who follow Jesus, and that includes you! From the Sermon on the Mount, Jesus said, *"Blessed are you when people insult you, persecute you and falsely say all kinds of evil against you because of me"* (*Matthew 5:11*). (Emphasis added.) On another occasion, Jesus concluded, *"I have told you these things, so that in me you may have peace. In this world, you will have trouble. But take heart! I have overcome the world"* (*John 16:33*). (Emphasis added.) Jesus promised there would be trouble in this life, but a glorious future awaits us. Paul echoes that statement in Romans 8:18. Thinking biblically, what does Jesus mean by *trouble* in John 16:33?

4. Concerning the suffering Paul referenced in Romans 18:18 and quoting from the *Theological Dictionary of the New Testament* "*that which befalls a man and has to be accepted by him. It also refers to the bodily or spiritual condition induced by external events: 'state of suffering,' 'sorrowful mood,' 'sorrow,' 'grief.' Rarely 'emotions.'*"

With that explanation of suffering in view, have not unexpected, uninvited, and altogether unwelcome things occurred in your life? Did you gracefully accept them as God's will for your life? Or, when suffering found you, was your response somewhat different? Did you ever say, "How can this be? How has God allowed this to happen to me? How can this _____ (tragedy, trial, crisis, death, illness, divorce, loss of employment, etc. – you fill in the blank) be good, lead to good, or come from God?"

If you've had these thoughts, you're not alone. Think biblically for a moment and consider how Joseph felt at the bottom of the well. What about King David? Out of fear for his life, he ran from King Saul and hid in a cave. How about Jonah? When he disobeyed God, He found himself in the belly of the whale. I wonder if they secretly asked questions like these?

Our definition of *suffering* from Romans 8:18 broadens our prospects for hardship and suffering in this life. We all struggle with something. What is the most pressing struggle in your life today? Are you prepared to stand still to see the salvation of the Lord?

5. Paul was no stranger to troubles like suffering and persecution. Perhaps he understood it, endured it, and glorified God through it better than most. Paul reported the following. "...five times I received forty *stripes* minus one. Three times I was beaten with rods; once I was stoned; three times I was shipwrecked; a night and a day I have been in the deep; *in* journeys often, *in* perils of waters, *in* perils of robbers, *in* perils of *my own* countrymen, *in* perils of the Gentiles, *in* perils in the city, *in* perils in the wilderness, *in* perils in the sea, *in* perils among false brethren; in weariness and toil, in sleeplessness often, in hunger and thirst, in fastings often, in cold and nakedness - ..." (2 Corinthians 11:24-27).

Thankfully, most of us will never know, experientially, the depth of Paul's sufferings for Christ for the benefit of the gospel. Yet, He proclaimed to them that it didn't matter. Hardship didn't stop him, nor did it change his focus or his mission.

    a. Read 1 Corinthians 2:2 to discover the depth of Paul's determination as well as his ultimate goal. Record the verse below.

b. Think biblically for a moment. In light of God's divine providence and His ultimate goal for all believers, what do you think was the purpose in Paul's suffering? Did God cause Paul's sufferings or merely allow them by His grace and for His glory? If possible, share a verse in support of your answer.

6. We must never forget that first-century Christians endured horrible persecution and injustice, including Paul and the disciples. Right after Paul escaped death from a brutal stoning, he returned to preaching and teaching. You might say, Paul was about the Father's business. His heart was always burdened to share the gospel of Christ and strengthen believers. In 2 Corinthians 11:28, Paul continued, "...besides the other things, what comes upon me daily: my deep concern for all the churches."

Acts 14 records that after being stoned, dragged out of the city, and left for dead, Paul got up and in the company of Barnabas, he departed to Derbe. When they arrived in Derbe, Paul set out again to strengthen the persecuted church. He feared no man and, indeed, not death. Paul didn't care if they stoned him again! He was on a mission from God, and he would rely upon God to see him through. That's where we all need to be. Are you there? Why or why not?

7. Do you have a "go-to" verse that encourages your faith when "troubles and suffering" come? If so, please record it below.

8. Read Acts 14:22. Luke's words reveal that Paul continued in the faith even through persecution. Notice that Luke's words echo Paul's message of Romans 8:17, which essentially says, "As heirs, who will share in His glory, we must also share in His suffering." For reinforcement, record Romans 8:17 below.

9. How are you doing? Have you been strengthened to be His witness and glorify Jesus during your trials or hardship? You are invited to share a bold testimony where your faith rose, and you met your trial with grace and strength in a way that honored God.

Trouble is not new to any of us. Our Lord Jesus promised that "troubles" would come. He never said "if" they come, instead "when" they come. From the following verses, we see that James, Luke, Peter, and Paul all promised trials and persecution, too. And their words proved right! Every disciple, except John, was martyred for his faith; it's the ultimate persecution. What was John's fate? He was boiled in oil and banished to the Island of Patmos. We have no record of his death, but we can assume that he died on Patmos at God's appointed time. That would be after he received and recorded the "Revelation" of God. Its twenty-two chapters are known as Holy scriptures and conclude the books of the New Testament.

10. The following verses address God's work of sanctification through our trials. Complete the passages below.

James promised:

James 1:2 "My brethren, count it all _____ when you fall into various _____,..."

Peter promised:

1 Peter 1:6 "In this you greatly _____, though now for a little while, if need be, you have been _____ _____ _____ _____...."

Paul promised:

Romans 12:12 "...rejoicing in _____, patient in _____, continuing steadfastly in _____;..."

Luke promised:

Acts 14:22 "...strengthening the souls of the disciples, exhorting *them* to _____ in the _____, and *saying*, "We must through many _____ enter the kingdom of _____."

From our text, Paul promised:

Romans 8:35 "Who shall separate us from the love of Christ? Shall _____, or _____, or _____, or _____, or _____, or _____, or _____?"

Sweet sisters, your suffering is not purposeless. You are being prepared for eternity through your trials. God is for you, not against you. He is always right, and is working all things together for good for those who love Him and are called according to His purpose. Can you see that the "good" in Romans 8:28 does not mean a "party" or "riches" in this world? The good that God had in view was conforming you/us to the image of His Son. This pruning will last a lifetime, and at times, it will be painful. But we must remember, it is nothing at all to be compared with our coming glory!

♥ Heart-Check For Today

11. As God's child, you are to give thanks for all things (Ephesians 5:20) and pray without ceasing (1 Thessalonians 5:16-18). Therefore, as we reflect on God's Word, it's time to give thanks to the Lord for your trials, tribulations, and momentary suffering. Rejoice! Through them, your Heavenly Father is fitting you for heaven and conforming you to the image of His Son. You are invited to close in prayer.

Knowing The Difference Between Trials And Temptation

A "temptation" is not to be confused with a "trial." By definition, a trial is a test of faith, patience, or stamina by suffering. In contrast, temptation comes from evil desires inside us and never from God. Scripture is clear on the matter. God does not tempt us. Temptation takes root with an evil *"thought"* and becomes a sin when we dwell on the *"thought"* and breathe life into it. Thereby, the *"thought"* becomes an action that will condemn us. In other words, the *"thought"* is not sinful, in and of itself, although Paul admonishes us to dwell on holy things, pure things, and good things, etc. Our trouble begins when we give life or energy to that *"thought"* by acting upon it or bringing it to life. Take note. If we give way to any passions or pursuits that are contrary to God's divine Word, it leads to sin every time. We know, too, sin's aim is death, not life!

We will conclude today's study by agreeing that God tests our faith, but never, ever does He tempt us or seduce us to sin. However, he will allow Satan to tempt or "sift" us to test and refine our faith through the sanctification process. God did it with Peter, and He will do it with us. A loving Father wants us to grow in our dependence on Him. So, too, He wants us to be like Jesus. Even today, He is working all things together for good because we love Him and are called according to His purpose.

Lesson 13: Future Glory and More Than Conquerors
Romans 8:18-39

Day Five: **Respond.** Review Romans 8:18-39

Memory Verse: "For I am persuaded that neither death nor life, nor angels nor principalities nor powers, nor things present nor things to come, nor height nor depth, nor any other created thing, shall be able to separate us from the love of God which is in Christ Jesus our Lord" (Romans 8:38-39).

We will conclude our study in Romans 8 with a look at our future glory and the rich promises of this amazing chapter. Review each verse and complete the associated promise.

We are promised:

1. In Romans 8:1 that there is no _____ for those who are in Christ Jesus.

2. In Romans 8:9 that if the Spirit of God dwells in us, we not in the _____, but in the _____.

3. In Romans 8:11 that through His Spirit who dwells in us, He who raised Christ Jesus from the dead will also give _____ to our mortal bodies.

4. In Romans 8:14 that all who are led by the _____ of God are _____ of God.

5. In Romans 8:26-27 that the Spirit makes _____ for the saints according to the _____ of God.

6. In Romans 8:28 that _____ _____ work together for _____ to those who love God, to those who are the _____ according to *His* purpose.

7. In Romans 8:29, that Jesus might be the firstborn among many brothers, that those He [God] foreknew He also _____ to be conformed to the image of is Son.

8. Romans 8:30 promised those whom He _____, He also _____; and those whom He called He also _____; and those whom He justified, He also _____.

9. In Romans 8:31 that if God is _____ us, no one can stand _____ us.

10. In Romans 8:33 that a charge against God's _____ shall not stand.

11. In Romans 8:37, we learned that through Him who loved us, we are more than "something." What are we?

12. In Romans 8:38-39, we learned what cannot separate us from the love of God. Prayerfully record Romans 8:38 and 8:39 below.

Romans 8:38

Romans 8:39

13. Look at this list. Is there any question about your security in God's love? God has poured out His love for us in Romans 8. Each of these rich promises has eternity in view. They positively affirm that God has good things in store for all those who have been called to faith in Christ. We are secure in the love of God. Sweet sisters, our coming glory is just ahead. Look up! Your redemption draws near! Of all the passages listed above, which one speaks to your heart most powerfully, and why? You are invited to share.

14. Paul provided encouragement concerning heaven and our future glory in Philippians 3:20. Read and review the passage. According to Paul, where is your citizenship?

15. The completed work of sanctification awaits us. Romans 8:18 references the resurrection of the body and the complete transformation into Christlikeness in our eternal glory. Absolutely nothing can compare to what awaits us. That's what we should hope and long for as children of God; to be like Jesus and to be with Him throughout eternity. Prayerfully read Philippians 3:21. What happens to our "lowly body" in Philippians 3:21.

16. Lastly, Paul has admonished believers not to focus on the suffering and troubles of this life. We must remember, this too shall pass because everything in this life will pass away. At long last, we will be in the presence of our Mighty King Jesus. In the blink of an eye, our troubles will be replaced with a crown. Look up, and praise God in your momentary suffering because our coming liberty is glorious! Prayerfully complete 2 Corinthians 4:15-18 below.

"For all things *are* for your sakes, that grace, having spread through the many, may cause _____ to abound to the glory of God. Therefore we do not _____ heart. Even though our outward *man* is _____, yet the inward man is being _____ day by day. For our light affliction, which is but for a moment, is working for us a far more exceeding *and* eternal weight of _____, while we do not look at the things which are _____, but at the things which are _____ seen. For the things which are seen *are* _____, but the things which *are* not seen are _____" (2 Corinthians 4:15-18).

In closing, let's review the glorious promise of our Weekly Memory Verse one last time. For its full impact, please read it aloud.

"For I am persuaded that neither death nor life, nor angels nor principalities nor powers, nor things present nor things to come, nor height nor depth, nor any other created thing, shall be able to separate us from the love of God which is in Christ Jesus our Lord" (Romans 8:38-39).

You are invited to close in prayer.

Words of Jesus
"Blessed are you when people insult you, persecute you and falsely say
all kinds of evil against you because of me" (Matthew 5:11).

Lesson 14: God's Sovereign Choice & Israel's Unbelief
Romans 9:1-33

Day One: **Read**. Prayerfully Read Romans 9:1-33

Memory Verse: "Behold, I lay in Zion a stumbling stone and rock of offense, And whoever believes on Him will not be put to shame" (Romans 9:33).

1. At the beginning of Romans 9, Paul makes a true confession. Review Romans 9:1-3 and answer the following questions.

   a. What two things were in Paul's heart.

   b. What did Paul wish, and on whose behalf?

   c. Using a dictionary or bible concordance, define *accursed*.

2. Review Romans 9:4. Paul's countrymen, according to the flesh, were Israelites. What six things pertained to them? Be specific.

_____

_____

_____

_____

_____

_____

3. Romans 9:5 links the Israelites to Christ. How so? To discover your answer, record Romans 9:5 below.

4. Read Romans 9:6. Although Israel rejects Christ, there is divine purpose in Israel's rejection. According to verse 6, was the "Word of God" ineffective? Yes or no?

5. Prayerfully complete Romans 9:6-7 below, beginning with the second sentence of verse 6.

"For they are not all _____ who _____ of Israel, nor are they all _____ because they are the _____ of Abraham; but..."

6. Thinking biblically, what is Paul saying about his countrymen, the Israelites?

7. Read and review Romans 9:7-9 and complete the passages, beginning with the second sentence of verse 7.

"... but, *In* _____ *your seed shall be* _____." That is, those who are the children of the _____, these are not the _____ of God; but the children of the _____ are counted as the seed. For this is the word of promise: "*At this time I will come and* _____ *shall have a* _____" (Romans 9:7-9).

8. Read and review Romans 9:10-13 and answer the following questions.

   a. According to Romans 9:10, Rebecca conceived through one man. Who was he, and how is he identified within the verse. Be specific.

   b. So that God's purpose in election *"might stand,"* His election rested on one twin and not the other. We see from Romans 9:11 that election was not of _____, but of Him who _____.

   c. How was God's choice of election revealed to Rebecca? Record Romans 9:12-13 below.

These are direct quotes from the Old Testament. Where have these words appeared before?

v. 12

v. 13

9. Thinking biblically, since the twins had not been born or had an opportunity to do good or evil, what stands out to you about election?

10. Think back to last week's lesson. What happened when God's electing love came to you?

11. Read Romans 9:14-15. Since there is no unrighteousness in God, how did God explain His mercy and compassion to Moses?

   a. Complete Romans 9:15 below.

"For He says to Moses, 'I will have _____ on _____ I will have mercy, and I will have _____ on whomever I will have _____,'" (Romans 9:15).

   b. ♥ <u>Heart-Check For Today</u>

The decision is God's – pure and simple. Stop a moment and consider the great gift God has bestowed on you. His electing love and grace (His unmerited, unearned favor) rest on you! He chose you before you were ever born, long before you were a twinkle in your dad's eye! God conceived you in his mind, called you, chose you, all before you were born. At the appointed time, God called you forth and introduced you to the world on the day of your birth! You're His creation, His masterpiece, His treasure, and His love. You're the object of His focus – always. That's regardless of how others see you, treat you, or think about you. And especially if and when you don't feel it. Know, today and always, that God's devoted and unfailing love and affection rests on you. Sweet sister, rejoice! You are the "elect" of God, and He created you on purpose – with purpose.

12. Romans 9:16 explains that God's mercy in election and salvation is not of two things, but instead of God's merciful choosing. It is exclusively God's divine choice to fulfill His eternal purposes. Identify the two things that have **no merit or standing** in election and describe what they mean.

   a.

   b.

Lesson 14: God's Sovereign Choice & Israel's Unbelief
Romans 9:1-33

Day Two: **Research**. Review Romans 9:1-33

Memory Verse: "Behold, I lay in Zion a stumbling stone and rock of offense, And whoever believes on Him will not be put to shame" (Romans 9:33).

I. Using a bible, bible dictionary, or concordance define the following **key words.**

covenants v. 4

mercy v. 15, 16, 18, 23

remnant v. 27

Sodom v. 29

Gomorrah v. 29

II. Read the following **key phrases.**

vessels of wrath v. 22 &

vessels of mercy, which <u>He had</u> prepared beforehand for glory v. 22 - Much debate has ensued through the ages about the phrase, "vessels of wrath prepared for destruction" in contrast with "vessels of mercy, which He had prepared beforehand for glory." Their meanings hinge on the interpretation of the original Greek language and the passive and active voice of the word "prepared" from each phrase. The question of debate becomes "*the who*" behind "*the preparation of the vessels.*"

From the first phrase, "***vessels <u>prepared for</u> destruction***," we find that the verb *prepared* is in the perfect tense and passive voice. That means the subject is the recipient of the verbal action, i.e., the *vessel* has received destruction or has accomplished destruction within itself. From the original language, there is no evidence of outside influence leading to destruction. We are quite capable of destruction within ourselves. All of humanity, apart from the Spirit of God, is despicable and capable of every evil imaginable and, sad to say, enjoying most of it.

Since all of humanity was made in the image of God and created for glory, we must pause to consider this predestined destruction. Since God did not make humanity for destruction, where's the disconnect? Simply stated, it's this. **When man rejected God, they, within themselves, sealed their fate.**

The broad meaning of "vessels of wrath" hinges on God's righteousness judgment in light of humanity's willful desire to reject Him in pursuit of evil passions and pleasures. Although it is no surprise to God, It appears that humanity is energized by evil. They may continue along this path for a season, but God will ultimately step in. Even though God is long-suffering, He will eventually give them over to themselves. (See Romans 1.) God is a just God, and those who reject Him will receive the justice they earn and deserve. The due penalty of their sins will visit them. In the end, all of humanity will "reap what they have sown," and because He is a God of mercy, everyone will be treated impartially. Those who embrace Him by coming to faith will receive mercy, forgiveness, and eternal life. True to His character, God is gracious, merciful, and long-suffering. Just so you know, that grace is the unearned, unmerited favor of God.

Dr. Warren Wiersbe expressed God's view of "vessels of wrath" as follows. *"We must never think that God enjoyed watching a tyrant like Pharaoh. He endured it. God said to Moses, 'I have surely seen the affliction of My people ... and have heard their cry ... for I know their sorrows' (Exodus 3:7). The fact that God was long-suffering indicates that He gave Pharaoh opportunities to be saved. (See 2 Peter 3:9.) The word 'prepared' [fitted, made for, predestined] from Romans 9:22 does not suggest that God made Pharaoh into a "vessel of wrath." According to Greek scholars, that verb form is in the passive or middle voice, making it a reflexive action verb. So, it should read: 'fitted himself for destruction.' God prepares men for glory (see Romans 9:23), but sinners prepare themselves for judgment. In Moses and Israel, God revealed the riches of His mercy; in Pharaoh and in Egypt, He revealed His power and wrath. Since neither deserved any mercy, God cannot be charged with injustice."* Record Exodus 9:16 below.

Exodus 9:16

Within the second phrase, ***"vessels He had prepared beforehand for glory"*** is somewhat different. Here, it appears in the aorist tense with an active voice. That means the verbal action is a "snapshot" event. It's an event that is portrayed as a state of being - without respect to any process. In other words, the *vessel* **has not** contributed to the process of being prepared beforehand for glory. How could we? Before God awakened our spirits, we were doing just the opposite. According to scripture, before salvation, we were God-haters, sinners, and vessels of wrath, working hardily to secure our destruction. Many scholars hold the opinion that the predestination of God is present in these verses. How so? Those who come to faith are moved from "vessels (objects) of God's wrath" to "vessels (objects) of His divine mercy." As salvation comes, they receive God's Spirit as well as God's divine mercy and all of its benefits in this life and the life to come.

As believers, we owe a tremendous debt of gratitude to God. Like Jacob, God chose you, called you, and saved you from before the womb. That was long before you could do anything good or evil. Thankfully, you had no part in it. **It was all God!** You didn't cause it or bring it about. So, in the mind of God, it was complete, accomplished, and a done deal long before the world began.

So we'll wrap this up by agreeing from start to finish, salvation is entirely a divine work of God. Apart from His electing love, we would never be saved. God has invited all who believe to take their position as "objects of His glory." That's *"the elect,"* and that includes you. How merciful! The *elect* consists of all those God chose before the foundation of the world to come to faith. In so doing, they become *vessels God had prepared beforehand for glory. Just think! As the elect, we are objects of His glory. How merciful of God to choose you as a vessel He prepared beforehand for His glory!*

"For whom He _____, He also _____ *to be* _____ to the image of His Son, that He might be the firstborn among many brethren. Moreover whom He _____, these He also _____; whom He _____, these He also _____; and whom He _____, these He also _____" (Romans 8:29-30).

stumbling stone v. 33 - One commentator said concerning the stumbling stone, "God gave the Jews a rock of foundation on which to stand and instead of standing on it, they fell over it." Consequently, all those of Zion who did not (and do not) trust in Jesus Christ (the cornerstone and foundation of the church and the rock of salvation) stumble. Although God pronounced judgment on Israel in Isaiah 28, He had prepared for them a way of escape. He would become their sanctuary, but Israel would stumble over it instead of embracing it and believing in it by coming to faith. Our merciful God lay in Zion a precious cornerstone so that whoever trusts in it would not be ashamed. (See Isaiah 28:18.) Therefore, all those who believe would be kept through judgment.

Paul assures believers throughout the New Testament that their faith would not disappoint. He assured believers they would not be ashamed or disappointed regarding their eschatological (end times) hope of salvation. The saved remnant of Israel would be saved or preserved like everyone else, by grace through faith. And to Paul, this faith was in the cornerstone, in Christ alone. Despite their rejection and denial of Christ, God remained faithful. Dr. Warren Wiersbe has noted that Romans 9 does not nullify Romans 8. In *The Bible Exposition Commentary*, Dr. Wiersbe said this concerning Israel's rejection of the cornerstone. "*God is still faithful, righteous, just, and gracious, and He can be depended on to accomplish His purposes and keep His promises.*" Record Isaiah 28:16. Underline what is said about the "*cornerstone.*"

Isaiah 28:16

rock of offense v. 33 - In v. 33, Paul reaches back to Isaiah 8:14 and 28:16 and combines their message. The prophets of old had said long before His (Christ's) coming that Israel would reject her Messiah. Although Isaiah had prophesied extensively throughout the southern Kingdom of Judah, his message was not received. Their rejection and unbelief have been consistent with the scriptures. In other words, the scriptures have been fulfilled in their unbelief and rejection of Christ, the cornerstone. Jesus is the foundation of the church and the rock of salvation. To most of Israel, "the rock of salvation" became a rock of offense.

The Greek-English Lexicon of the New Testament states the following concerning Isaiah 8:14 stumbling stone reference. "*'Stumbling stone and rock of offense' - an obstacle on the path over which one falls. It can also mean the 'cause of the disaster.'*" That means the obstacle on the path - the rock of offense - would lead to their ruin. But watch this. The Jews' rejection and "stumbling stone" made way for salvation to the Gentiles by God's grace and His ultimate glory. Later in Romans 11, we shall see that their rejection had a divine purpose and benefited us. Some scholars conclude, "By God's grace, they [the Jews'] were blinded for our sake."

Lastly, their rejection kept them in sin. Rejecting Jesus keeps all of us in sin. It is a great offense that leads to our ruin. All those who reject Jesus will suffer the harsh consequences of their sins. All unconfessed, unrepentant sin leads to destruction and ultimately death, but the sin which seals man's eternal fate is the greatest sin of all. That would be the rejection of His Spirit and Jesus Christ as Savior.

Isaiah 8:14

Romans 11:11

Lesson 14: God's Sovereign Choice & Israel's Unbelief
Romans 9:1-33

Day Three: **Receive**. Review Romans 9:1-33

Memory Verse: "Behold, I lay in Zion a stumbling stone and rock of offense, And whoever believes on Him will not be put to shame" (Romans 9:33).

1. Read and review Romans 9:17. What does God announce to Pharaoh concerning His power and its purpose?

2. Romans 9:17 parallels Exodus 9:16. For comparison, please read and record Exodus 9:16.

3. Paul concludes with a powerful statement in Romans 9:18. Summarize the passage below.

You had absolutely nothing to do with your conception and birth. You had nothing at all to do with your rebirth, either. When God's electing love rested on you and called you to faith, it was entirely His doing. There is nothing you could ever do to earn God's favor. You didn't earn it, you didn't buy it, and you can't change it. As always, God will have mercy on those He chooses. (See Romans 9:15.) Those He chooses will come to faith and call upon the name of the Lord.

There is no unrighteousness in God or His plan to save man; like His nature, His plan is all good! We owe our thanks to God! A merciful Father is still saving to the uttermost by His grace and for His glory. Stop for a minute and consider these words. God desires that no man perish, and He has called you, just as you are, to faith in Christ alone.

4. Review Romans 9:17. What did the Scripture speak to Pharaoh? Be specific.

5. We have no influence over God; we never have and never will! Paul refuted such skewed thoughts with the words of Isaiah. (See Isaiah 29:16 and 45:9.) Essentially, these passages ask, "Doesn't the potter have authority over the clay?" The meaning of these words was not new to the Jews. Review Romans 9:19-21 and answer the following questions.

    a. Prideful humanity has not only questioned God's existence but His authority as well. Too, they have clung to sin and, in unbelief, ignored God. Through their decline, many have concluded and confessed, "There is no God." Paul calls them out! They are not ignorant, merely willful. What crucial question does Paul pose in the first phrase of Romans 9:20?

    b. What question does Paul ask in the second phrase of Romans 9:20? Be specific.

    c. Review Romans 9:20. From Paul's analogy of the potter and his clay, we see the intimacy of God's intentional *"hands-on"* work in our lives. His work in and through us is not only intentional but it's rooted in love and a desire for fellowship with us. After all, God individually created us for a unique relationship with Him and to bear His image. Note, too, that God has never turned His back on humanity, nor will He. Instead, He has upheld and sustained us from the garden, even though we have sometimes pushed against His grace, and some have rejected Him altogether. Do you recognize God's tender care and intentionality in your life? Or, have you ever asked, "God, how could you make me like this, or for this purpose?"

    d. Review Romans 9:21. What happens from the same lump of clay? Be specific.

6. Review Romans 9:22-24 and answer the following questions.

    a. From the first phrase of Romans 9:22, what was God planning to do concerning his wrath and power? Complete the phrase. The verse begins, *"What if God,...*

    b. What does long-suffering mean? Does it describe you?

    c. Review Romans 9:23. God planned to put His glorious mercy on display. Which vessels would God use? When were they prepared?

    d. Review Romans 9:24 and identify *"even us whom He called."* Who has God called?

7. Read and review Romans 9:25-29 to complete the passages.

    v. 25 "As He says also in Hosea: 'I will call them My _____, who were not My _____, And her_____, who was not _____.'

    v. 26 And it shall come to pass in the place where it was said to them, 'You are not My _____,' There they shall be called _____ of the living God."

v. 27 Isaiah also cries out concerning Israel: 'Though the number of the children of Israel be as the _____ of the _____, the _____ will be _____.

v. 28 For He will finish the _____ and cut it short in righteousness, Because the Lord will make a _____ _____ upon the earth.'

v. 29 "And as Isaiah said before: 'Unless the Lord of Sabaoth [Sabbath] had left us a _____, We would have become _____ Sodom, And we would have been _____ _____ Gomorrah' " (Romans 9:25-29).

8. Justification by faith was a rock or offense – a stumbling stone - to the Jews. Paul brings Romans 9 to a close as he sums up Israel's spiritual condition. Read and review Romans 9:30-33. In your own words, outline the main point(s) of verses 30 – 32 below.

v. 30

v. 31

v. 32

9. Paul concludes the chapter referencing another familiar message to the Jews. Drawing from the prophet's words of Isaiah 8:14 and 28:16, Paul concludes his powerful message.

v. 33 "As it is written: 'Behold, I lay in Zion a _____ _____ and _____ of _____, And whoever _____ on _____ will not be put to _____.' "

Before you close in prayer, review God's merciful promise and rejoice! You owe all your praise and thanks to God. You're invited to close in prayer.

Lesson 14: God's Sovereign Choice & Israel's Unbelief
Romans 9:1-33

Day Four: **Reflect**. Prayerfully Review Romans 9:1-33

Memory Verse: "Behold, I lay in Zion a stumbling stone and rock of offense, And whoever believes on Him will not be put to shame" (Romans 9:33).

As you reflect on Chapter 9, you might wonder, "Did God chose the wrong people? What happened to the Israelites, the descendants of Abraham through Jacob, whose name was changed by God to Israel?" The name change alone is quite significant. God had declared through covenantal promises that the Israelites were His chosen people. Before the foundation of the world, God's sovereignty had selected an entire nation to receive His special calling, covenant promises, and blessings. They were to *consecrate themselves unto God and be His witness to all the nations.* God had told Abraham, "…And in you all the families of the earth shall be blessed" (Genesis 12:3). God had promised Abraham that He would bless those who blessed Abraham and curse those who cursed him.

We must take note. With this great privilege of call came responsibility, but for the most part, these chosen ones failed. Instead of embracing God's call and living heavenward, and trusting in God to deliver them, they rejected His grace repeatedly. Collectively, they served the righteousness of the law instead of embracing and serving the law of grace. What does that mean? Simply this. It was easier to "work" their way to God and "get-her-done" themselves (by working to earn God's favor) than to trust in the One who had done it all and prepared the way. They already had God's favor – He had called and chosen them, for goodness sake! Believing was so simple that it became too difficult and elusive. In some measure, this was their stumbling block. The Jews could work tirelessly – they are hard workers and doers - but they couldn't believe a little, even as much as a mustard seed seemed to be unattainable.

Moving forward, we must ask ourselves, "Am I trusting in my good works, or by faith, in Christ alone?" How could they believe it was easier to strive and work to keep the commandments plus 613 laws from the Talmud (the oral law or rabbinical teaching) rather than believing in God? To all but the remnant, works trumped faith!

Let's review God's to Israel. Read Isaiah 46:1-4 and answer the following questions.

1. Look closely at the verses. Who is doing the work? _____

2. Complete God's promise from Isaiah 46:3-4 below.

v. 3 "Listen to Me, O house of Jacob, And all the _____ of the house of _____, Who have been _____ by Me from _____, Who have been _____ from the womb:

v. 4 Even to your old age, _____ _____ _____ And even to gray hairs _____ _____ _____ _____ ! _____ have made, and _____ will bear; Even _____ will _____, and will _____ you" (Isaiah 46:3-4).

3. These passages reflect the covenantal promises of God. Remember, a covenant was God's legally binding promise that could not be overturned, overruled, or broken. It was similar to a legal agreement or contract of today, but as we all know, people break promises all the time. The courts are full of lawsuits involving broken contracts. God, however, is a promise keeper! There are six biblical covenants in scripture. A list is provided at the end of this lesson. Make it a point to review the promises of God. The same God who called and chose Israel upholds His Word today. One bible scholar noted, "All but one of God's covenants with man are eternal and unilateral. That is, God promised to accomplish something based on His character and not on the response or actions of the promised beneficiary."

4. Their rejection made way for the salvation of the Gentiles. Read and record Romans 11:11 below.

Romans 11:11

5. Was this a mistake? Certainly not! God knew all along they would reject Him. He is sovereign and omniscient. The prophet Jeremiah promised a *new covenant*. Read Jeremiah 31:31-33. According to these verses, what was God's plan? Be specific.

6. Although God's chosen rejected Him; He remained steadfast to His nature and character. All that He promises is secure. Only The Mosaic Covenant was not eternal and unilateral. Because of Israel's sins, God repealed it and replaced it with the New Covenant. Bible scholars agree that the New Covenant is the secret to the believer's empowered life. To discover God's abundant provisions through the New Covenant, read and review Hebrews 8:7-13 below.

Hebrews 8: 7-13 "For if that first covenant had been faultless, then no place would have been sought for a second. Because finding fault with them, He says: *'Behold, the days are coming, says the Lord, when I will make a new covenant with the house of Israel and with the house of Judah - not according to the covenant that I made with their fathers in the day when I took them by the hand to lead them out of the land of Egypt; because they did not continue in My covenant, and I disregarded them, says the Lord.* For this is the covenant that I will make with the house of Israel after those days, says the Lord: I will put My laws in their mind and write them on their hearts; and I will be their God, and they shall be My people. *None of them shall teach his neighbor, and none his brother, saying, 'Know the Lord,'* for all shall know Me, from the least of them to the greatest of them. For I will be merciful to their unrighteousness, and their sins and their lawless deeds I will remember no more.' In that, He says, 'A *new* covenant,' He has made the first obsolete. Now what is becoming obsolete and growing old is ready to vanish away" (Hebrews 8:7-13).

7. Review the verses above and underline the irrevocable *I will* promises of God. How many do you discover?_____

8. In your own hand, please prayerfully record Hebrews 8:12 below.

9. The Israelites rejected God's (free and unprecedented) gift and attempted to earn their salvation instead. As you review Hebrews 8:12, consider all God has accomplished on your behalf through His Son Jesus. He has done so based on His nature and character, not because of you, instead, despite you. When we believe, we receive mercy, although according to Paul's words of Romans 3:23, we fall painfully short according to God's holy standard. Take the time to review the promises of God in scripture. Record a scriptural promise that repeatedly gives you hope and strength. You are invited to share.

God has promised me:

You are invited to close in prayer.

FYI: Bible Covenants

The Noahic Covenant - Genesis 9:8-7

The Abrahamic Covenant - Genesis 12:1-3

The Mosaic Covenant - Unlike other covenants, the Mosaic Covenant was a conditional covenant of works. According to 2 Corinthians 3:7-9, this covenant was a ministry of "condemnation" and "death." The covenant was to reveal Israel's sin, God's remedy, and ultimately lead the transgressors to Christ. The Mosaic Covenant is spread throughout many passages of scripture. In addition to being spread throughout scripture, *New Unger's Bible Handbook,* reports that the Mosaic Covenant is revealed in Exodus 20:1 through Exodus 31:18. Within these passages, the covenant includes giving to the Ten commandments, judgments, and the religious ordinances.

The Priestly Covenant - Numbers 25:10-13

The Davidic Covenant - 2 Samuel 7:8-16 - the covenant of the eternal kingdom

The New Covenant - Jeremiah 31:31-35; Ezekiel 37:26; and Hebrews 8:7-13.

When God Changes A Name, It Changes Everything!

From *The Exhaustive Dictionary Of Bible Names,* we find:

"**Jacob** (ja'-cub) - He will supplant; he that supplants; he that follows after; a heeler; one who trips up; takes hold by the hand; supplanter; a ***deceiver***, a detainer."

Additionally, from the *Baker Encyclopedia of the Bible,* we find additional information concerning Jacob's name. It states, *"Jacob was born holding the heel of his brother so that he was named Jacob, 'he takes by the heel,' referencing Hosea 12:3, with the derived meaning 'to supplant, **deceive**, attack from the rear.'"* For clarity, record Hosea 12:3 below.

Hosea 12:3

Take note. When God changed Jacob's name to Israel, He also changed his identity. God used a name change to transform Jacob from a "man of deception to a man who was ruled by God." That's a picture and type of all who wrestle with God and come to faith. You once were full of deceit, and now you are led and governed by God. The definition of Jacob's new name, Israel, is provided below. It's quoted from the *Exhaustive Dictionary Of Bible Names.*

"**Israel** (iz'-ra-el) - He will be a prince with God; prince with God; contender of God; he strives with God; soldier of God; God will rule; ***God-ruled man***; ruling with God; one that prevails with God."

Lesson 14: God's Sovereign Choice & Israel's Unbelief
Romans 9:1-33

Day Five: **Respond**. Review Romans 9:1-33

Memory verse: "Behold, I lay in Zion a stumbling stone and rock of offense, And whoever believes on Him will not be put to shame" (Romans 9:33).

1. Read and review Romans 9:22-24. Take note of God's mercy within these verses - His mercy is immense! Its depth and magnitude are far greater than we can comprehend. Although we don't "long-suffer," well, God is other than us! He will endure with much long-suffering, the "vessels of wrath prepared for destruction." How long will He endure? He will endure until the appointed time when His work has been accomplished, and His purposes are fulfilled. From Romans 9:22, we see that God had two purposes for enduring with much long-suffering. What were they?

    a. to show_____

    b. to make_____

2. Paul concludes this section with a rhetorical question in Romans 9:23-24. In Pauline fashion, the Old Testament scholar answers his question through the prophetic words of Hosea. Read the verses below and underline all the words that position you as "sons (daughters) of the living God."

v. 25 "As He says also in Hosea:

'I will call them My people, who were not My people,

And her beloved, who was not beloved.' "

v. 26 "And it shall come to pass in the place where it was said to them,

'You are not My people,'

There they shall be called sons of the living God."

Again, in Romans 9:25-29, Paul skillfully reaches back to the Old Testament prophets to recall God's work of salvation. His purpose was two-fold. First, as a reminder that saving the Gentiles was always part of His redemptive plan. And next, to remind them that a remnant of Jews will come to faith.

3. Review Romans 9:25-26. Paul uses the prophet Hosea to reinforce God's choice. From these passages, who is doing the calling? _____ Does it appear that these receiving God's call have earned it or participated in God's choice? Yes or no?

4. With divine purpose, God will call those that are not his people *"my people,"* and those who are not beloved *"beloved."* God had revealed His plan to call Gentiles to faith even though they were strangers to the covenant. Remember, all of us were once "far off" and strangers to the covenant. Mercifully, God does not save sinners based on their good works or ethnicity. Nor does He save based on wealth, performance (behavior), beauty, or intellect. And that's a good thing! That, alone, should give you cause to rejoice! **God's purpose in election makes it possible for anyone He chooses to be saved by grace through faith.** Think about it. People from every tongue, tribe and nation are called, chosen, justified, and, ultimately, will be glorified – including you.

Remember, too, that salvation is always a permanent holy work – a divine spiritual work through which God gives us life and seals us with His Spirit as a guarantee. It's God's plan from eternity past, it cannot be hindered or stopped, and it can only come from Him. Read Revelation 5:9. Complete the passage below.

"And they sang a _____ song, saying: '_____ are _____ to take the _____, And to _____ its seals; For _____ _____ _____, And have _____ us to God by Your _____ out of every tribe and tongue and people and nation,...' " (Revelation 5:9).

5. That is the church, Christ's bride, called to be sons of the living God. Peter also echoes the prophetic words of Hosea in 1 Peter 2:9-10. Through these passages, Peter highlights the privileges of New Testament believers. Through faith in Christ, our inheritance is secure. We shall be called *"sons of the living God,"* for we have obtained mercy. Complete the comforting words of 1 Peter 2:9-10 below.

"But you *are* a _____ generation, a _____ priesthood, a holy nation, His own _____ people, that you may proclaim the _____ of Him who called you out of _____ into His marvelous _____; who once *were* not a people but *are* now the_____ of _____, who had not obtained _____ but now have obtained _____."

6. In Romans 9:27-29, we see that Paul's attention turns back to the plight of the Jews. In recalling God's promises, the prophetic words of Isaiah come to mind, and Paul quotes from Isaiah 10:22-23. Although they (the Jews) had rejected their promised Messiah, a remnant would be saved. Look closely at what Paul is saying. Only a remnant would remain (come to faith or be saved) from a people who were once counted "as numerous as the sand of the sea."

God has always had a remnant. These were His chosen people, and from them, a remnant would remain. Review Romans 9:28. Thinking biblically, what particulars are shared concerning God's work on earth in Romans 9:28? Be specific.

7. At the appointed time, God worked His redemption plan through His Son Jesus, a descendant of the house of David. It fulfilled the Davidic covenant of 2 Samuel 7:8-16. By God's grace and for His glory, sons of the living God would include Jews and Gentiles. Salvation comes from God alone, and birthright has nothing to do with faith. We are not born Christians, and as Paul pointed out, all Jews *"are not Israel because they are of Israel."* God was pleased to bless all those who placed their hope and trust in God's plan for redemption, the promised Messiah, who takes away the sins of the world. Record Romans 9:6 below.

Romans 9:6

8. All salvation comes by grace through faith. Read and record Ephesians 2:8-9 below.

"For by _____ you have been saved through _____, and that not of _____; *it is* **the gift of God,** not of _____, lest anyone should boast" (Ephesians 2:8-9) (Emphasis added).

9. We are saved when God is pleased to reveal His Son in us. It occurs when we are spiritually awakened to receive God's spirit, simultaneously coming to faith and confessing Christ Jesus as Lord and Savior. This confession must include repenting of sin (agreeing with God and turning away from sin) because there is no salvation without heartfelt repentance. (Please note concerning repentance. True repentance embodies agreement with God and His Word. That means seeing sin as God does and moving away from it. That's everything that pushes against His Word and moral standards, including thoughts, words, actions, or deeds.) For clarity, read Galatians 1:15-16, wherein we find a portion of Paul's conversion testimony and answer the questions below.

   a. What immediately comes to mind from these verses?

   b. Who did the work?

   c. What was Paul's part in it?

Not to oversimplify, but because God's spiritual work in salvation is so important, let's look again. When it pleased God to reveal His Son in Paul, he was awakened spiritually and believed - coming to faith in Christ alone. One Bible scholar stated concerning Paul's conversion, *"Not only was Christ revealed to Paul on the Damascus Road, but in him, as God gave him the life, light, and faith to believe in Him."*

As you can see, although Paul's election was from eternity past, he didn't know it. That is until the appointed time. What time was that? When it pleased God (and for eternal purposes), His Spirit was not only given to Paul but revealed (awakened, made known) to Paul as well. As he was born of God's Spirit, he was called from death to life. God's Spirit took up residence in him and witnessed with Paul's spirit that he was God's child. Instantly, Paul was a new man in Christ.

That's precisely how it happened in us. One moment you believed, but in all the moments before, you didn't! At the precise moment that God had planned, and when it pleased Him, He awakened you (and Paul, and all other believers) spiritually, and you/they believed by coming to faith in Christ.

So, What Of The Jews?

You may be wondering, "What of the Jews - the chosen people of God?" Chapter 11 will answer the remaining questions concerning the plight of the Jews and God's final plan. Rest assured, God has not forgotten the Jews! He is merciful and long-suffering and desiring that no man perish!

10. Before we respond in prayer, read and review Romans 9:30-33. It is faith, and faith alone, that brings us into the family of God. We are daughters because of God's grace, which called us to faith. Israel rejected God as a nation, although a remnant was secure. Their rejection made way for the Gentiles. What the Jews were too religious to receive, we received by faith, with awe and wonder. What a plan! What an amazing God! We believe because it has been His plan from before the foundation of the world. Record Romans 9:33 below.

Romans 9:33

You are invited to close in prayer. Please pray for Israel, the Jews, and the peace of Jerusalem.

Words of Jesus
"From that time Jesus began to preach and to say, 'Repent,
for the kingdom of heaven is at hand' " (Matthew 4:17).

Lesson 15: The Jews Rejection of Christ
Romans 10:1-21

Day One: **Read**. Prayerfully Read Romans 10:1-21

Memory Verse: "For the Scripture says, 'Whoever believes on Him will not be put to shame' " (Romans 10:11).

1. Review Romans 10:1. What was Paul's heartfelt desire and prayer for Israel?

2. From Romans 10:2, what did they (the Jews) have for God that was not according to knowledge?

3. Review Romans 10:3. What two things prevented them from submitting to the righteousness of God?

   a.

   b.

4. Review Romans 10:4. Who is Christ to everyone who believes? Be specific.

5. Read Romans 10:5 and Leviticus 18:5. In both passages, Moses writes about the righteousness of the law.

   a. In Romans 10:5, Paul quotes Moses' words from Leviticus 18:5. Record Leviticus 18:5 below.

   b. In light of both passages, what two things were required of "man?"

6. Read and review Romans 10:6-7. Thinking biblically, what does it mean to a.) *"bring Christ down from above,"* and b.) *"bring Christ up from the dead?"*

   a.

   b.

7. Review Romans 10:8-9 and complete its promise below.

"The _____ is near you, in your _____ and in your _____" (that is, the word of _____ which we preach): that if you _____ with your _____ the Lord Jesus and _____ in your _____ that God has raised Him from the _____, you will be _____" (Romans 10:8-9).

8. What is Paul's explanation from Romans 10:10?

9. a. Read and record the scriptural promise from Romans 10:11 below.

   b. According to the verse, who is identified as the recipients of God's unfailing grace?

10. Read and review Romans 10:12 and answer the following.

   a. According to Paul, why is there no distinction between Jew and Greek?

   b. Thinking biblically, what verb describes the Lord's response to both the Jew and Greek?
   _____

11. Rejoice! The Lord *is rich* to all who call upon Him. Read and review Romans 10:13. What is the Lord's response to all who call upon Him? What is the promised result?

Lesson 15: The Jews Rejection of Christ
Romans 10:1-21

Day Two: **Research**. Prayerfully Read Romans 10:1-21

Memory Verse: "For the Scripture says, 'Whoever believes on Him will not be put to shame' " (Romans 10:11).

I. Using a bible, bible dictionary, or concordance define the following **key words.**

submitted v. 3

abyss v. 7

preach v. 15

confess v. 9; *confession* v. 10

provoke v. 19

disobedient v. 21

contrary v. 21

II. Read the following *key phrases.*

their own righteousness v. 3 - The Jews desired righteousness before God, but they wanted to obtain it on their terms. In other words, they wanted to have "right standing" before God through works, personal merit, and keeping the law rather than by faith. They are not alone in their thinking. Some folks never embrace the simplicity of the gospel and instead miss out because they believe they must "be good or do good" to be part of God's kingdom.

The Bible identifies two types of righteousness: 1.) *works righteousness,* which comes from keeping the law, and 2.) *faith righteousness, which* is God's gift to all who believe. Since what we believe determines who we are, how we live, and where we will spend eternity, let's take a closer look.

While *works-righteousness* is performance-based and suggests that we can earn our right standing before God, faith-righteousness calls us to believe in what God has accomplished on our behalf. Notice the stark contrast between working and believing! Jesus explained to "a certain ruler" who had inquired about the way to salvation, "The things which are impossible with men are possible with God" (Luke 18:27). Salvation is a spiritual work that only comes from God. You can't earn it, buy it, or perform well enough to receive it. And that's a good thing because how would we ever be sure we have done enough. Instead, God has done it all on your behalf. All you need is the faith to believe, and even that is a gift from God.

So, why was this so hard for the Jews? Part of their dilemma was rooted in "doing or working" instead of "resting or believing." For the most part, they were oriented towards *works-righteousness, which was learned behavior passed from father to son from generation to generation.* With a performance-based mindset inspired by many years of tradition and ceremonial actions, *faith-righteousness* eluded them. It seemed too easy to be true. Years of do's and don'ts had burdened them into thinking that they could earn God's approval through good works, good behavior, and religious rituals. So, in their zeal for God, **they worked** rather than having faith in Him. Interestingly, their errored thinking not only afforded them striving and toil but piety as well. They believed they played a part in salvation, which leads to self-righteousness and spiritual blindness.

What's righteousness? One Bible scholar described it as the state or condition of perfectly conforming to God's law and holy character. Simply stated, righteousness is right standing before God, and it's only available by God's grace through faith. When we come to faith, God imputes His holy righteousness to us. That's the divine act of ungodly sinners being made holy and perfect in the eyes of God. So, faith not only saves us, but it's pleasing to God as well. Prayerfully read and record Hebrews 11:6 below.

Hebrews 11:6

the righteousness of God v. 3 - God's very nature and character set the standard for righteousness. Righteousness is God, and all righteousness comes from God. It is consistent with every aspect of His character and nature. It has never changed and never will. It is not impacted by man or influenced by any outward force. The righteousness of God is embedded in Him. He always acts righteousness, and all He determines is just. He is always Godly, and it would be impossible for Him to be otherwise, for He cannot be separated from His character and nature. He is, at all times, found in the state of righteousness.

We obtain the righteousness of God by faith. A textbook definition for righteousness would be *the state or condition of perfectly conforming to God's law and holy character*. Although we fall painfully short in our humanness, His righteousness is imputed to us when we believe or come to faith. In an instant, we are born of God's Spirit. From that moment on, although humanly speaking, we fall far short - we are righteous in the sight of God. Only God is inherently righteous, and only He can make us righteous too. Read Deuteronomy 32:4 and Matthew 5:48. Complete the words of Jesus from Matthew 4:48 below.

"Therefore you shall be _____, just as your Father in heaven is _____" (Matthew 5:48).

word of faith which we preach v. 8 – Literally, the "message of faith which we proclaim." The message of faith is our gateway to God. The truth of the gospel of Christ is what we believe and what we proclaim. According to the *Greek-English Lexicon of the New Testament*, "*to preach is: to publicly announce religious truths and principles while urging acceptance and compliance.*" Read Deuteronomy 30:14 and answer the following questions.

    a. Where is the word?

    b. For what purpose?

gospel of peace v.15 - The "good news of peace." The only real and lasting peace comes from Jesus, our Prince of Peace. True peace is found in Christ alone, who leads us into peace. From the *Greek-English Lexicon of the New Testament*, "*the gospel of peace is communicated as 'the good news,' with particular reference to the good news about Jesus. To communicate [teach, deliver] the gospel of peace is 'to tell the good news, to announce the gospel.'*"

We must grasp the full meaning of biblical "*peace*" to understand this verse. The *Theological Dictionary of the New Testament* states concerning peace, "*The basic feature of the Greek concept of 'peace' is that the word does not primarily denote a relationship between several people, or an attitude, but a state [condition, position, circumstance], such as a 'time of peace' or 'state of peace.' Peace was initially conceived [envisioned] of like an interlude in the perpetual state of war.*"

From the *Theological Dictionary of the New Testament*, we read. "*With 'messengers of peace,' bearers of 'good news,' peace is synonymous with salvation and victory. These divine announcements may be eschatological or reference the end times because they link justice, peace, and salvation. Some of these messages are messianic. (That means some of these divine announcements point expressly to the Messiah.) For example, "The government will rest upon his shoulders; or his name will be called ... Prince of Peace. For the growth of his government and peace will be without end." The death of the Messiah/liberator will be expiatory (it will atone for guilt and sin): "The punishment that earned our peace [salvation] has fallen upon him (the Servant of Yahweh)." (See Isaiah 53:5.)*

New Testament writers would recognize that religious peace was accomplished only through Jesus. To Paul, the gospel of peace includes the believer being at "peace with God." That comes from our faith in Christ Jesus, which makes us righteous in the eyes of God and gives us peace in our hearts and souls. This peace affords you the surety that you're His child, forgiven and reconciled to Him. You know and enjoy salvation and await with confidence for your eternal glory. Complete Ephesians 2:13-18 below.

"But now in _____ _____ you who once were far off have been brought _____ by the _____ of Christ. v. 14 For He Himself is our _____, who has made both _____, and has broken down the middle _____ of _____, v. 15 having abolished in _____ flesh the _____, *that is,* the law of commandments *contained* in ordinances, so as to create in Himself one _____ _____ *from* the two, *thus* making _____, v.16 and that He might reconcile them _____ to God in one _____ through the _____, thereby putting to death the enmity. v. 17 And He came and **preached** _____ to you who were afar off and to those who were near. v. 18 For through _____ we _____ have access by one _____ to the Father" (Ephesians 2:13-18).

From these verses, can you identify who was far off and who was near?

   a. far off _____

   b. near _____

obeyed the gospel v. 16 - There is a command in the gospel message. It is much more than a gracious offer. It is a command to repent and believe. The gospel message is indeed good news, but it has always demanded a decision. The gospel's desired end is that we repent and believe. Apart from repentance, there is no salvation. Record 2 Thessalonians 1:7-8 below.

v. 7

v. 8

Lesson 15: The Jews Rejection of Christ
Romans 10:1-21

Day Three: **Receive**. Review Romans 10:1-21

Memory Verse: "For the Scripture says, 'Whoever believes on Him will not be put to shame' "

(Romans 10:11).

1. Review Romans 10:14-15. Paul asks four important questions in this verse. Record the main point of each question.

   Question one:_____

   Question two:_____

   Question three:_____

   Question four:_____

2. In Romans 10:15, Paul, an Old Testament scholar, quotes Isaiah's words (Isaiah 52:7), referencing those who would preach the gospel. Isaiah used these beautiful words to stress the significance of those messengers who brought news concerning Israel's imminent release from Babylonian captivity. Read and review Isaiah 52:7 and complete the original passages below.

   How _____ upon the mountains

   Are the _____ of him who brings _____ _____,

   Who proclaims_____,

   Who brings _____ _____ of _____ *things,*

   Who proclaims _____-,

Who says to Zion, "_____ _____ _____!"

3. Review Romans 10:16-17. They have not all obeyed the gospel!

   a. For Isaiah says:

   b. How does Isaiah report that faith comes? Be specific. Record Romans 10:17 as your answer.

4. Read and review Romans 10:18. Scripture always confirms scripture. In verse 18, Paul reaches back to Psalm 19 to affirm that the heavens declare the glory of God. In essence, Paul says, "indeed, surely, most definitely they have heard!" The Israelites would have no excuse because scripture confirms the gospel had been proclaimed to every creature under heaven.

   a. What has gone out to all the earth? v. 18

   b. And, what to the ends of the world? v. 18

5. What question does Paul ask concerning Israel at the beginning of Romans 10:19?

6. Paul draws upon Moses' testimony in Deuteronomy 32 concerning the methods God sometimes employs to carry out His divine purposes. In the passage below, Moses declares that God had used another nation to move Israel to anger. For your answer, complete Romans 10:19 below.

"I will provoke you to _____ by those who _____ _____ a nation, I will move you to _____ by a _____ nation."

7. Thinking biblically, what was God's ultimate purpose concerning Israel? If possible, record a passage of scripture in support of your answer.

8. Read Romans 10:20-21. Again, Paul reaches back to the Old Testament. Verses 20-21 convey the prophet's message from Isaiah 65:1-2. In boldness, what did Isaiah proclaim? Read and record the words of verse 20 below.

v. 20

♥ Heart-Check For Today

9. From before the foundation of the world, God planned to save you! Did you seek after God? Did you ask for Him? Prayerfully review the words of Romans 10:20, and complete the sentence below. You are invited to share.

The Lord has loved me, (your name)_____ from eternity past with an everlasting love and as a result, I

10. Read and review Romans 10: 21. God's arms are outstretched "all day long" as He awaits Israel's response. In the wait, how does God describe Israel?

_____ and _____

11. Can you imagine how God must feel since His chosen has rejected Him? You are invited to close in prayer. As you pray for the peace of Jerusalem, remember God's unfailing love for the Jews. Ask God's Spirit to move upon their hearts and save the lost souls of Israel.

Lesson 15: The Jews Rejection of Christ
Romans 10:1-21

Day Four: **Reflect**. Prayerfully Review Romans 10:1-21

Memory Verse: "For the Scripture says, 'Whoever believes on Him will not be put to shame' " (Romans 10:11).

All who call upon the name of the Lord will be saved. Our memory verse promises, "Whoever believes on Him will not be put to shame." God is the God of every man, and He is still saving to the uttermost. John 3:16 assures, "For God so loved the world, that he gave his only begotten Son, that whosoever believeth in him should not perish, but have everlasting life" (KJV). What a rich promise! Do you see any qualifiers in that verse? There is one; it's *"whosoever believes."* That's it, pure and simple – that's the gospel! Anyone who believes and calls upon the name, Jesus, is saved and becomes a child of God. All their sin debt is paid in full (including its eternal consequences), and their status is forever changed. Immediately, they have a new identity, destiny, and access to God. It doesn't matter who you are, where you've been, or what you've done in the past – even moments before salvation. What a gift, you're forgiven, and your history is irrelevant; God remembers it no more. Instantly, there is no record of any wrong concerning you! With God, it's all about the future - your future in Him. When you come to faith, you become the forgiven child of the King and a co-heir to all that our God Most High can give!

God loves you, and He created you for fellowship with Him. You must remember that even though humanity is the pinnacle of all that God created, we often appear weak and act frail, as evidenced by our actions, mistakes, and missteps. Even so, God has got your back; He is for you and not against you! God not only knows your current circumstances - good or bad, but what it will take to claim your heart and the moment you will come to faith.

Our God is faithful. He has been so since the garden. Let's pause a moment to explore the shepherd's story from Luke 2. Through it, we can see God's faithful love and tender mercies. Today's lesson will take us on a brief detour back to Jesus' birth in Bethlehem. Carefully review these passages as we take the shepherd's lives and God's plan into account. God loved the shepherds, as He loves us. Even today, He is "loving" sinners into His kingdom. That includes the least and the lost, youngest and weakest, marginalized and forgotten, and the most infirmed - wherever they are found. It included these shepherds too! Remember, no one is beyond God's reach and His unfailing love.

As we pull back the curtain on Luke 2, we find that the shepherds were busy doing the "shepherd-thing," and they thought it was a typical night - like all others - and it was until it wasn't. Out of the darkness, "...behold, an angel of the Lord stood before them, and the glory of the Lord shone around them, and they were greatly afraid" (Luke 2:9).

This night was quite ordinary until they received God's angelic messenger heralding news of the Christ-child born in Bethlehem. Up until that moment, they never knew they were on God's radar. They lived and worked in isolation - among their flocks - without community or fellowship. Too, they were ceremonially unclean because their "hands-on" work with sheep involved close contact with blood and other bodily fluids, which rendered them unclean. So, shepherding was lonely work, but it was more than that. Since life and death hung in the balance, at times, shepherding was messy. But guess what? God called them too! Even though they were unaware, God's keeping eye was upon them; likewise, it's upon you as well.

What happened next? The shepherds heard and received the good news and were compelled to go to Bethlehem. It happened just as God planned. After seeing the Christ-child, they worshipped and praised God. Then, they departed and testified of Jesus and on His behalf. They were the first of all God's image-bearers to worship, praise, and adore Jesus. How thrilling it was for them! God had called unclean men of no reputation to be the first to come and see His child – the Lord Jesus - as He lay in a manger. But it's much more than that. He called them to proclaim the "good news," and they were the first to do so.

Prayerfully Read Luke 2:8-20 and answer the following questions.

1. Do you think the shepherds felt like God had forgotten them? In our humanness, sometimes we feel alone and forgotten. But guess what? The eye of God was on the shepherds. Even in the dark of night in Bethlehem, the watchful eye of God was not eclipsed. Do you ever feel like He has forgotten you? You are invited to share about a time when you felt that God had forgotten you.

2. God will never leave you or forsake you. You are in His heart and on His mind. He has good things planned for you because you are His child. If you are waiting on a scriptural promise from God, He will bring it about at the appointed time. Read Romans 8:28 and summarize it below.

3. In 1990, Garth Brooks wrote a country song titled "Unanswered Prayers!" It took the country music charts by storm during 1991. The song's central theme was gratefulness because God had not answered some of his prayers. It still happens, you know. When we pray, sometimes, we don't get the response we desire. But, we must praise Him anyway - remembering that God's divine wisdom knows best! His answer is always timely and perfect for every situation. You're invited to share about a time when God said, "No!" to your request, and instead, gave something not only good or better but best, instead!

Read and review Romans 10:10-13 and answer the following questions.

4. Salvation from start to finish is a spiritual work of God. But this does not exempt us from the responsibility of believing and confessing our faith.

"For with the_____ one _____ unto righteousness, and with the _____ confession is made unto _____" (Romans 10:10).

5. Have you made a public confession of faith in Christ for salvation? Yes or no?

Do you recall the date and time? If so, record it here. _____

6. The shepherds shared publicly, and the Bible says, others "marveled" in awe of their testimony. God used shepherds to herald the "good news" even though their testimony would not be permissible in court. How amazing is that? God not only called them to witness the amazing miracle of Jesus' birth, but He elevated their status and gave them a voice! A voice to praise Him, worship Him, and proclaim Jesus has come! They not only saw, they believed. What was their testimony? Simply this. "The King is born in Bethlehem and is laying in a manger."

Until their eyes were opened, they had nothing to share. It's the same with us. Before we believe, there's not much worth sharing. But when faith awakens us, the "good news" is everything! Are you born again? Do you share your story? If not, pray for the boldness of the shepherds. What have you got to lose? They were the most unlikely of all to be believed. But guess what? Folks marveled! Moreover, told listened and believed! We should follow their lead by stepping out in faith, sharing the gospel's good news, and leaving the results to God. If you've already done so, please share the results below.

7. Review this week's memory verse, which reads, "For the Scripture says, 'Whoever believes on Him will not be put to shame'" (Romans 10:11). There's a qualifier within the verse? Do you see it? Identify it, and underline it within the passage.

8. From Romans 10:11, what "rich" promise is given, and what does "rich" mean?

9. Review Romans 10:12. Is there a distinction between Jew and Gentile? Why or why not?

10. In Romans 10:12, we read, "...the same Lord over all is _____ to all who call upon Him." In this verse, *"rich"* means giving generously. Has not God been generous to you? The shepherds experienced a marvelous life-changing blessing from God. In an instant, God elevated their status and changed their destiny. Most assuredly, when they encountered the miracle of Jesus, they believed. As a result, they praised and worshiped Him.

Have you not benefited richly from calling upon Him? Of course, you have! Please share your shortlist of "rich" benefits below. Record them in the order of their importance.

11. Record the rich promise of Romans 10:13 below.

Romans 10:13 –

Read the words that you just wrote from Romans 10:13. Nobody is beyond the reach of God's love. Nobody is too unclean, too untrustworthy, or too sinful to be saved by the blood of Jesus. To be saved, you must believe in your heart and confess with your mouth that Jesus Christ is your personal Lord and Savior. It has been said of the one who believes. "It is stating his belief by his mouth that confirms his salvation."

12. When you consider Romans 10:13, what does it speak to you about God's love? What one word comes to mind? _____

13. Jesus promises that **all** who come will be received. Read John 6:37-40.

"All that the Father gives Me will come to Me, and the one who comes to Me I will by no means cast out. For I have come down from heaven, not to do My own will, but the will of Him who sent Me. This is the will of the Father who sent Me, that of all He has given Me I should lose nothing, but should raise it up at the last day. And this is the will of Him who sent Me, that everyone who sees the Son and believes in Him may have everlasting life; and I will raise him up at the last day."

God is faithful. You will not be put to shame.

14. Review John 6:37-40 above, and answer the following:

   a. Underline the words or phrases of God's faithful promises through Christ Jesus in these passages. (See John 6:37-40 above.)

   b. Review the passages. How do believers come to Jesus?

Notice that we can't come to Jesus apart from God's plan. "All that the Father gives Me will come to Me..." (John 6:37). God still does the choosing. That's His plan, and that's His electing love at work to call forth the church - His church. Is there someone in your life that needs Jesus and salvation? Pray that God will woo them by His spirit and call them to faith in Christ alone.

You're invited to write their name(s) here:_____

As you close today's lesson, would you hold them before God's throne of grace? Remember, He desires that none perish, but that all come to saving faith instead. God is still in the business of winning souls for His kingdom, building His church, forgiving all sins, and preparing His bride for eternity.

Lay your petition at His feet as you come boldly into His presence. Be encouraged, whoever they are and whatever they've done, the blood of Jesus is more than enough to save them and cleanse them of all unrighteousness! All the "whosoever's who believe" and call upon the name shall be saved! Trust Jesus. His eye was on the shepherds, and He called them. His eye is on your loved ones, and He can call them too!

Lesson 15: The Jews Rejection of Christ
Romans 10:1-21

Day Five: **Respond**. Review Romans 10:1-21

Memory Verse: "For the Scripture says, 'Whoever believes on Him will not be put to shame' " (Romans 10:11).

Yesterday's lesson ended with us kneeling at the throne of grace, asking Jesus to save a loved one(s), a neighbor, friend, co-worker, etc. We were laboring in prayer for "the lost" to be saved. When we pray in this way, we partner with God in His work of salvation. Today, we will conclude our study of Romans 10 with an examination of God's Word in the work of winning souls for the Kingdom. Our text comes from Romans 10:14-17.

> "How then shall they call on Him in whom they have not believed? And how shall they believe in Him of whom they have not heard? And how shall they hear without a preacher? And how shall they preach unless they are sent? As it is written:
>
> 'How beautiful are the feet of those who preach the gospel of peace, Who bring glad tidings of good things!'
>
> But they have not all obeyed the gospel. For Isaiah says, 'Lord, who has believed our report?' So then faith comes by hearing, and hearing by the word of God."

These passages are recognized as the premise behind the call of missionaries, teachers, pastors, and workers of the faith who labor among "the lost" to be God's witness. If you're saved, you're called to be His witness, too. The call of the Church comes from Acts 1:8. If you're unfamiliar with this passage, please review it now.

Missionaries and teachers, etc., can be foreign or domestic. Many serve in the country of their origin. Others forsake everything and travel far from home to distant parts of the world. There, like Abraham, they become strangers in a foreign land. Before going, many learn new languages and others study medicine and nursing. Others, having the knowledge or training to build and staff hospitals or schools, do. Even still, other missionaries unite to pray for a harvest and plant churches to disciple, encourage, and grow Christ's Church at home and abroad.

From the beginning, although locations and times have changed, the call has remained the same. God called Abraham in Genesis 12. He called my husband and me in 2004. Astoundingly, Abraham and Sarah went, and we went too! It continues. He is still calling and sending. After all, God is a missionary God; He sent us Jesus! Saving souls is the desire of His heart as it has been from the beginning. God has always desired to have a people set apart for fellowship with Him, obey Him, worship Him, and follow Him. Remember, the chief end of man is to glorify God and enjoy Him forever. When we think of female missionaries, women like Amy Carmichael, Elizabeth Elliott, or Mother Teresa might come to mind. Before we move ahead, let's pause a moment to take a brief look at Mother Teresa's missionary life.

If you're unfamiliar with her story, Mother Teresa was a nun who labored tirelessly among the poor in Calcutta, India, in association with the Catholic Church. She owned next to nothing and feared absolutely nothing - no man or illness - not even AIDS when it ravaged thousands in Calcutta during its height of epidemic rampage. As a result of her sacrifice, many souls were added to the Kingdom. Although she never asked for recognition, in 1997, she was elevated to the status of Saint Teresa by the Catholic Church. Mother Teresa loved people - period! Her love was an extension of God's unfailing love. Daily, she became His hands and feet while loving the sick and diseased, those you might consider unlovable or untouchable. But not to Mother Teresa. Her most passionate desire was that no one perished separated from God, fearful, alone, or in shame. She held countless dying victims just before they crossed over into eternity. We can only imagine that many came to faith in those last moments of their earthly life. No doubt, God used her loving embrace and passionate pleas to fill His Kingdom.

Suffice it to say, these Christian laborers, like Mother Teresa, all hold the distinction of being called by God and anointed by Him for a particular work. Only God can shape a missionary heart, a pastor's heart, a worship leader's heart, a Bible teacher's heart, etc. He does so with purpose and eternity in view. Interestingly, Christian laborers come from every corner of the globe. They're not unique or special in God's eyes, but their message, call, and unique gifts are. What sets them apart? The same thing that sets all great communicators apart. It's their message, of course, and their God-infused call to share it! These communicate the best story ever told!

It has been said of former President Ronald Regan that "He was a great communicator." His humble response, "I'm not a great communicator; I just communicate a great message." It's the same with missionaries. They have the privilege of sharing God's truth – the good news – the gospel of God. They build a bridge or platform for communication such as a school, a church, a hospital, a Zumba or yoga class, a soup kitchen, or a clothes closet, etc., and use that bridge to connect people and build relationships. Essentially, they meet a need. And when those in need come, they're loved and served faithfully. As trust is established and at the appropriate time, they're told the best news of all – the gospel! What news could be better than "Jesus has come, has died for humanity's sins, and loves them not as they should be, but just as they are!

So, what sets all believers, including missionaries, apart? It's the message - the story they tell! Remember Paul? God saved him, filled him, and fitted him for service. God provided all that Paul needed for success. Ultimately, he had no choice but to obey because God's electing call is irresistible. God's workers labor tirelessly by His grace and for His glory, with one unified message – the gospel – which is powerful and effective unto salvation. It's the focus or backdrop of today's lesson. Paul assures, "For '*whoever calls* on the name of the Lord shall be saved' " (Romans 10:13). So, what's the good news?

Simply stated, it's this. Jesus came to save sinners and saves all who call upon the name of the Lord. He is an equal opportunity Savior and will save all who come! The only qualifier is faith! God loved the world, not just people who look like you and me. One day we will see the rainbow of heaven, His bride, God's church, shoulder to shoulder praising our great God, Savior, and King Jesus. What a sight that will be, the beautiful people of God from every tongue, tribe, and nation in a hallelujah chorus that will last throughout eternity! He is still calling and sending workers to reap His harvest. Pray for the harvest! Even today, God is saving and forgiving, and until the mountains melt like wax, God's work of saving souls will continue.

1. Read and review Romans 10:14-17. The message must be proclaimed! Apart from hearing God's good news (the Word), there is no salvation. How can people believe in a stranger - of someone whom they've never heard?

A messenger must go and proclaim the good news. It all begins with God's call. If He doesn't call, no one goes, if no one goes, no one preaches, if no one preaches, no one hears, if no one hears, no one comes to faith, if no one comes to faith, no one calls upon the name of Jesus, and if no one calls upon the name of Jesus, no one will be saved. It's just that simple. One scholar noted concerning these verses, *"the essence of Paul's argument is seen if we put his six verbs in the opposite order: Christ sends heralds; heralds preach; people hear; hearers believe; believers call; and those who call are saved."* Thinking biblically, does another scripture come to mind that confirms Paul's words of Romans 10:14-17.

2. Paul borrowed from Isaiah, the Old Testament prophet when he penned Romans 10:14-17. Isaiah 52:7 originally referenced Israel's imminent release from Babylonian captivity. Paul has aptly used it to reference the "apostolic bearers" of the message of the gospel. It is still the same today. In Romans 10:14-15, "preaching" was the focus. It highlights those called and anointed to speak and teach on God's behalf for the souls of men. Do you recall the first time you heard the gospel message? It was good news! Was it not? You are invited to share.

Salvation could not have happened apart from God's word. The two work hand in hand. God's Spirit awakens our spirit so that we can hear the truth of the gospel. Only the believer can hear, and those who hear believe!

3. From these passages, we'll conclude that faith is awakened by the message. Only God's Spirit can birth His Word in our hearts and call us to faith. Without the power of His Spirit, the Word is

ineffective. Romans 10:14-21 deals with Israel's rejection of the gospel even though a remnant always remains. They heard the same gospel message as the Gentiles, yet, many of them rejected it.

Thinking biblically, what do you think happened to the Jews? Find your answer within chapter 10. In your opinion, which group of passages best highlight the willful ignorance of Israel's unbelief even though the scriptures they loved and cherished contained God's salvation truth?

♥ Heart-Check For Today

For whom will you pray? Below is the name of my person or people. A word of caution is needed concerning prayer. Don't spread yourself too thin. Laboring in prayer for the souls of others should not be entered into lightly, and it takes perseverance and time. Start with a small list and then expand it as praying for others begins to feel natural. When you meet with Jesus, pray that He will burden your heart to labor effectively, consistently, and with sincerity of heart. In this work, we truly co-labor with Christ!

My person/people:

4. Next, since "faith comes by hearing and hearing by the word of God," are you prepared to share the gospel? If you are saved, you are called. Acts 1:8 the call of Christ'sChrist's church. Collectively, we are called to be His witness. If we do not go, how will they hear? And if we do not share, how can they come to faith? Without faith and repentance, there can never be salvation. With those thoughts in mind, what would God have you to do?

Think prayerfully about this. Many are not saved, possibly within your reach. Is there someone in your sphere of influence that needs Jesus? Have you shared with them the miracle of God's forgiveness and plan for salvation? Have you told them how much God loves them? Pray for the opportunity. Pray that God's Spirit will go before you to prepare their heart(s) to hear His word. Remember, faith comes by hearing and hearing by the word of God.

Prayerfully make a plan. (A suggested model is found below.) Next, please share it with others. Ask them to join with you in prayer for your words and the salvation of those who hear them. Then, commit it all to God in prayer. And last, wait on God's timing.

You will know when the opportunity comes. His Spirit will lead and guide you in the process. If you don't get the results you had hoped, keep praying, and don't despair; trust them to God. He loves them far more than you do, and He desires that people come to faith. A seed has been planted, pray that someone else will water it, and one day, a harvest will surely come. Only God knows their timing. Remember, all of humanity is on a collision course with God. When they encounter His irresistible love by the Spirit's power, they will surely know it and receive Jesus into their hearts.

A. Make your plan, and then commit it to prayer. Remain open and flexible; God may make changes. We can make a plan, but only God can bring it about. (Some examples of plans might include: When, where, and how often you will pray. Also, what scripture you will read before and afterward, or not. Will you fast before prayer? Will you invite others to pray with you or, instead, get into your prayer closet alone.) You determine. God will give you wisdom and insight. Take note. Over time, you may need to adapt your plan as God nudges you to make changes. So, be open and prepared to adjust your prayer time as His Spirit so moves.

My initial plan:

B. Pray on their behalf. Unburden your heart before God for their souls. He is waiting to hear from heaven and answer your prayers.

C. Invite a co-laborer to pray. I have asked _____ to partner with me in prayer for _____'s salvation.

(Note: A co-laborer does not necessarily warrant in-person praying. For example, my prayer partner and I have lived in separate cities and sometimes countries since 2007.)

D. **Lastly, pray and wait.** Timing is everything. We are always in a hurry, but God is not. When He opens that door, you'll be ready to share the "good news" because He is faithful. What a privilege it is to share the truth of the gospel of Christ. From start to finish, it is the most beautiful story ever told. Be bold in your endeavor, like the shepherds, "...glorifying and praising God for all the things they had heard and seen, as it was told them." Luke 2:20.

Words of Jesus
"This is the will of the Father who sent Me, that of all He has given Me I should lose nothing, but should raise it up at the last day" (John 6:39).

Lesson 16: Restoration - The Remnant Of Israel & Ingrafted Branches
Romans 11:1-36

Day One: **Read**. Prayerfully Read Romans 11:1-36

Memory Verse: "For the gifts and the calling of God are irrevocable" (Romans 11:29).

Read and review Romans 11:1-12 and answer the following questions.

1. In Romans 11:1, Paul speaks of his birth origin. Paul comes from what seed and what tribe?

2. Review Romans 11:2. Has God cast away His people?

3. Elijah plead with God against Israel. What did he pray? Read and record Romans 11:3 as your answer.

4. God answered Elijah. What is God's divine response in Romans 11:4?

"I have reserved for Myself _____ _____ men who have not bowed the knee to Baal" (Romans 11:4).

5. Thinking biblically, what might the phrase "not bowed the knee to Baal," mean?

6. Paul insists that a remnant is chosen by grace and not by works. v. 6. Be specific.

    a. When is grace no longer grace?

    b. When is work no longer work?

7. We are saved by grace through faith. Read and record Ephesians 2:8-9 below.

    v. 8

    v. 9

8. What then? Three things occurred in Romans 11:7. List the occurrences below?

    a.

    b.

    c.

9. Review Romans 11:8-10 and complete the following quotes from the Old Testament.

v. 8 "Just as it is written: 'God has given them a spirit of _____, Eyes that they should not _____ And _____ that they should not _____ To this very day.' "

v. 9 "And David says: 'Let their table become a _____ and a _____, A _____ block and a _____ to them.' "

v. 10 "Let their _____ be darkened, so that they do not _____, And _____ _____ their back always."

Note: Throughout the remainder of Romans 11, we shall discover God's purpose in the work of salvation for both the Jews and the Gentile. Israel's rejection is not final. He has reserved a remnant, and by His grace and for His glory, the chosen people of God will not be left out. Our merciful God will see them through. Of course, God has a plan for Israel!

10. Review Romans 11:11. The Jews stumbled!

   a. Through their fall, what was provoked? _____

   b. What came to the Gentiles as a result of the Jews' fall? _____

11. Their fall was their fullness! Read and record Romans 11:12 below.

Romans 11:12 –

12. Read Romans 11:13. Notice that Paul spoke with authority. How has Paul identified himself in this passage, and what does that mean?

13. Had Israel's unbelief led to their absolute ruin and destruction? Paul didn't think so. He believed that the Jews' apostasy or stumbling was not final. He knew that God would not forsake His chosen people. Why? Because a faithful God had promised Abraham that every nation, that's "all the families of the earth," would be blessed in the blessing of Abraham.

As we bring today's lesson to its end, let's explore God's promise to the Jew and Gentiles from Galatians 3:28-29. Prayerfully complete the passage below.

Read Galatians 3:28-29. Complete the promise Paul shared with the Galatians.

"There is neither _____ nor _____, there is neither _____ nor _____, there is neither _____ nor _____; for you are all _____ in Christ Jesus. And if you *are* _____, then you are _____ Seed, and _____ according to the promise" (Galatians 3:28-29)

Lesson 16: Restoration -
The Remnant Of Israel & Ingrafted Branches
Romans 11:1-36

Day Two: **Research**. Review Romans 11:1-36

Memory Verse: "For the gifts and the calling of God are irrevocable" (Romans 11: 29).

I. Using a bible, bible dictionary, or concordance define the following **key words.**

remnant v. 5

grace v. 5, 6

stupor v. 8

haughty v. 20

irrevocable v. 29

unsearchable v. 33

II. Read the following **key phrases.**

election of grace v. 5 – includes all those elected or chosen by God's grace to believe. That's all those chosen by God's grace for salvation, those who would come to faith in Christ. Notice that God's choice cannot be separated from His grace. Those He chose or elected to believe have received God's grace. Grace is God's unearned, unmerited favor. Believers are not saved because of what they have done. Instead, you have been saved by His choosing and mercy.

"Isaiah also cries out concerning Israel: 'Though the _____ of the children of _____ be as the sand of the sea, The _____ will be _____.' " (Romans 9:27).

partaker of the root v. 17 - The partners, participants, sharers of the root (of Abraham), the holy root of Israel. From the *Greek-English Lexicon of the New Testament*, *"Romans 11:28 proves that Paul is thinking of the fathers – the holiness of the patriarchs - which is the basis [foundation] of Israel's existence. They [Israel] from the very first were chosen and fashioned by God with a view to the work of salvation accomplished in Christ."* Romans 11:28 reads in part, *"...but concerning the election they are beloved for the sake of the fathers."* Note: God had made Abraham a promise, and to that, He would be faithful. Also, please note that God chose Israel for this express purpose – by His grace and for His glory. It was wholly a work of grace from the beginning. They had no impact on God's decision. Absolutely nothing in Israel purposed God to choose them. Read Romans 4:16 and summarize it below.

fatness of the olive tree v. 17 – A literal reading of Romans 11:17 from *the Greek-English Lexicon of the New Testament*, which states, *" 'of the root of the richness.' Fatness means a nutritionally rich, fatty quality—'fatness, rich quality.' The root of the fatness or richness refers to the healthy, nutritionally sound root which produced good olives, which in turn yielded much oil."*

natural branch, branches v. 21, 24 - From this parable (Romans 11:16-24), the natural branches represent God's chosen nation - Israel. It must be noted that chapter 11 is not personal **rather national.** In this sense, it references people collectively, the nation of Jews, and everyone else, otherwise known as the Gentiles. The Jews, the natural branch, enjoyed a rich spiritual heritage, but they would be "cut off" or "broken off" for their apostasy or unbelief.

In the parable, Paul describes a cultivated olive tree hosting natural branches that were not bearing fruit. These non-productive branches were cut off. Bible scholar, pastor, and author R. C. Sproul noted this concerning the parable. *"But the tree was not left in that condition, or it would be disfig-*

ured and become stunted in its growth. God's work is not merely to cultivate by cutting off the dead branches, but by grafting new branches on to the tree. Paul says 'A wild olive shoot has been joined to it.' "

Who is the wild olive shoot? The Gentiles who enjoy the benefits of the rich spiritual heritage and "fatness" of the olive tree by God's grace and for His glory! God purposed to have a tree that bore fruit for the kingdom, and He would have it indeed. The tree, His church, consisting of all believers, makes up the family of God. We all draw strength from the "root" - the forefathers of the faith. Today, the church stands upon the shoulders of Old Testament saints who have died in faith, looking forward with anticipation to the promised Messiah. In faith, we look back to Jesus and the cross and forward, by faith, to all the promises of God, to the revelation of the sons of God, and Jesus' second coming. Read and record Romans 8:18-19 below.

v. 18

v. 19

continue in His goodness v. 22 - In balance and perfect harmony, our loving God saves and executes justice. He rules and reigns in the fullest sense. He forgives sins and saves to the uttermost while holding the unjust accountable for their sins. One day all the injustice of this world will be vindicated by our fair and just creator and ruler of the world. One day soon, every knee will bow to Jesus, and every tongue confess to God! (See Romans 14:11.) As believers, we must continue in "His goodness," relying wholly upon what He has accomplished on our behalf and never boasting that we have attained something in and of ourselves that was beyond the Jews' reach. It is by God's grace, mercy, and "His goodness" that we stand. We are justified in the sight of God because we have believed! Pure and simple, God has done it all. From start to finish, salvation is the divine work of God. According to Ephesians 2:12, the Gentiles were foreigners and strangers to the covenants of the Old Testament. Read Ephesians 2:12-13. Complete verse 13 below.

"But now in Christ Jesus you who once were _____ off have been brought near by the _____ of _____" (Ephesians 2:13).

fullness of the Gentiles v. 25 - the number of Gentiles God chose to call to faith. The fullness refers to the accomplishment of all who come to faith during the Church age. According to Paul Benware, author of *Understanding End Times Prophecy*, the Jews' have been cut off temporarily. He wrote, *"One theme of Romans 11 is that, when the Jewish people rejected Christ, they were temporarily cut off from the blessings of a relationship with God. As a result, the gospel was given to the Gentiles, and they gladly received it. This partial hardening of heart for Israel doesn't preclude individual Jews from being saved, but it prevents the nation from accepting Christ as Messiah until His plans are finished. When the time is right, God will restore the entire nation, and they will come to faith in Him once again, ending "the times of the Gentiles."*

Matthew Henry, a beloved scholar from the past, has written the following concerning Romans 11:25-32. *"Of all judgments, spiritual judgments are the sorest; of these, the apostle is here speaking. The restoration of the Jews is, in the course of things, far less improbable than the call of the Gentiles to be the children of Abraham. Though others now possess these privileges, it will not hinder their being admitted again. By rejecting the gospel, and by their indignation at its being preached to the Gentiles, the Jews were become [sic] enemies to God; yet they are still to be favored for the sake of their pious fathers. Though at present, they are enemies to the gospel, for their hatred to the Gentiles; yet, <u>when God's time is come, [sic] that will no longer exist, and God's love to their fathers will be remembered.</u> True grace seeks not to confine God's favor. Those who find mercy themselves should endeavor that through their mercy, others also may obtain mercy." (Emphasis added.)*

Read and record Paul's warning from 1 Corinthians 10:12 below.

So, What About The Jews?

As we bring today's lesson to a close, rejoice! Our faithful God has not forgotten the Jews.

Conservative Bible scholars consider the verses of Romans 11:25-31 to be the most important in scripture concerning the future restoration of the Jews to Christ. What of the Jews? Will they come to faith? Within these passages, we find our answer.

When the fullness of the Gentiles is accomplished, the Jews will be saved. God always had a plan to save His people. He has not forgotten them, nor will He forsake them. What kind of hope could we have in Christ's promises if He would forsake or abandon the initial recipients of His divine mercy and grace?

Rest assured, our faithful God will not leave them like they are. He will call them to faith at the appointed time by His grace and for His glory!

Lesson 16: Restoration -
The Remnant Of Israel & Ingrafted Branches
Romans 11:1-36

Day Three: **Receive**. Review Romans 11:1-36

Memory Verse: "For the gifts and the calling of God are irrevocable" (Romans 11:29).

Since the beginning of Romans 9, the dominant theme or focus of Paul's writing has been the condition of Israel - the plight of the Jews. Conservative commentators agree that Paul was talking about the Jews but most assuredly writing to the Gentiles. Consequently, He was addressing those God had called him to reach and serve.

1. Review Romans 11:13-15. Who does Paul confess to being, and how did he plan to magnify his ministry? v. 13

    a. Paul was_____

    b. Paul planned_____

2. Who was cast away, for what purpose, and what would their acceptance be? v. 15

    a. Who:_____

    b. What:_____

    c. Their acceptance will be:_____

3. Review Romans 11:16-22 and answer the following questions.

    a. Why are the branches holy?

    b. Who is identified as a wild olive tree?

c. Who is grafted in, and how are they supported?

d. How should those "grafted-in" respond? Record Romans 11:19 as your response.

Romans 11:19 -

e. Why were they broken off, and how do we stand? v. 20

f. Record Paul's warning in the last phrase of v. 20.

g. Read Romans 11:21. Did God spare the natural branches? Circle Yes or no? Will He spare you? _____

h. Review Romans 11:22. From this verse, concerning the "goodness and severity" of God, which has He extended to you? Circle your response.

i. Read and review v. 22. God's goodness was conditional, and a warning followed.

    The condition:

The warning is found in the last phrase of v. 22. Record it below.

v. 22 -

4. Thinking biblically, what does it mean to "*continue in His goodness*"? Please record a verse of scripture in support of your answer.

5. Review Romans 11:23-27 and answer the following.

   a. What is promised Romans 11:23? To whom is it promised?

   b. In your own words, share the meaning of Romans 11:24 below.

   c. Who are the "natural branches," and who is their "own olive tree"?

6. Complete the passages from Romans 11:25-27.

"For I do not desire, brethren, that _____ should be _____ of this mystery, lest you should be wise in your own opinion, that _____ in part has happened to _____ until the _____ of the _____ has come in. 26 And so all _____ will be saved, as it is written:

    'The _____ will come out of _____,
    And He will turn away _____ from Jacob;

For this is My _____ with them,
When I take away their _____ '" (Romans 11:25-27).

7. Review the passages you just completed. God always had a plan for Israel. He did not forsake the Jews!

    a. Who is the Deliverer to come out of Zion? _____

    b. Who made a Covenant to take away their sins? _____

8. What is said concerning the gospel in Romans 11:28? Be specific.

9. Prayerfully read and record the promise of Romans 11:29 below.

Romans 11:29 -

10. What does the promise of verse 29 mean to you? You are invited to share.

11. God is merciful! First, read and review Romans 11:30-32. Then, in your own words, share the main point(s) of each verse.

v. 30

v. 31

v. 32

12. How amazing is our God! Paul concludes chapter 11 joyfully praising the wonderful works of God and His plan of salvation. Cheerfully complete Romans 11:33-35 below.

"Oh, the depth of the riches both of the_____ and _____ of God! How unsearchable are His _____ and His ways past finding out! For who has known the _____ of the Lord? Or who has become His _____? Or who has first _____ to Him And it shall be _____ to him?"

13. What can we give to God? Only our wholehearted faith. He has called us to faith and asked that we believe in Christ alone. We owe our thanks to God, for He has done it all. Sweet sisters, it has never been about what we can do, rather about what our amazing God has done on our behalf. Paul concludes chapter 11 with his spirit soaring! As you receive God's word into your heart, you are invited to record your prayer of praise and thanksgiving below. Please include Paul's words from Romans 11:36 at the end of your prayer. You are invited to record your prayer below.

Mighty and gracious Heavenly Father,

v. 36

Lesson 16: Restoration -
The Remnant Of Israel & Ingrafted Branches
Romans 11:1-36

Day Four: **Reflect**. Prayerfully Review Romans 11:1-36

Memory Verse: "For the gifts and the calling of God are irrevocable" (Romans 11:29).

Lessons four and five are centered on God's faithfulness and His purpose in the work of salvation despite man's arrogance, apostasy, and unbelief. His plan has not changed, nor has He forgotten His promises. He will be faithful to save "whoever calls upon the name of the Lord." (See Romans 10:13).

In Romans 11, Paul assures that "a faithful remnant remains." (See Romans 11:5.) A remnant, however, represents only a scant portion of those "called by God." One cannot help but wonder what will become of the Jews? God chose them. They were His first choice, but as a nation, they despised and rejected Jesus. You will recall. At the height of their fear and loathing, a Jewish mob of brothers held a "kangaroo" court to condemn their King. When they were offered His freedom, they chose to release Barabbas instead and crucified our Lord Jesus, the Passover Lamb. But first, they beat Him beyond recognition and crowned Him with a diadem of thorns. Finally, with great fanfare and hatred in their hearts, they placed His cross upon His bloody shoulders and paraded Him outside the gates of the city. On Golgotha, they hung Him on a tree between two common thieves until it was finished and complete. How long did it take? Until the purposes of God were accomplished and the prophecies fulfilled. If they had not nailed Jesus to the cross, His love would have held Him there. On the cross overlooking the city and people that Jesus loved, the depravity of man collided with God's unprecedented love. At the time appointed by God, our gracious Lord despised the shame, and as His final act of earthly love, He looked down from the cross and forgave the enemies of God. How profound! His passionate love for all men is without end, even these.

Throughout the church-age, questions concerning the Jews have remained. For example, "When and how will the Jews be brought in? Will the nation be saved? If so, will they be of more value to God than us? What is the fullness of the Gentiles, and how will it all be reconciled? Has the New Covenant Church replaced the Jews as the chosen people of God?" And lastly, "If God could forget them, what does it say about His promises to us?"

Scripture records concerning election and the Jews, "they are beloved for the sake of their fathers." (See Romans 11:28.) And our memory verse assures, "the gifts and the calling of God are irrevocable." (Romans 11:29). From the *Theological Lexicon of the New Testament,* we find God's faithfulness at the core of His irrevocable call. It reads, "*God does not change His mind; once God has chosen His people, He will not go back on the decision; God never breaks His word after making a promise.*" Reading from the *Theological Dictionary of the New Testament,* "*He (God) has in view the inflexible goal that in spite of the disobedience and hardness of men, He will accomplish His will to save.*"

Therefore, undergirding His irrevocable call, we find that God's faithfulness and the reliability of His promise are based on His divine character and nature. God will save all those who are His not because of us but despite us. God is forever faithful to His purpose.

God cannot and will not forget the Jews, and neither should we. The family of God, His Church, stands upon the shoulders of the Jewish saints who have travailed with God before us. Remember, Abraham was called, and as he responded, God began to record His faithful dealings with all who come to faith. In fact, Abraham believed God, and it was credited to him as righteousness. The faith of Abraham is the standard by which all faith is judged. Through Abraham and his descendants, the march of the faithful is recorded in scripture. Much rich tradition has come from the Jews, and the Old Testament is replete with the promise of Jesus, and it supports and upholds all that the New Testament reveals. From Genesis to Revelation, God's Word is an increasing unveiling or revelation of our Lord and Savior Jesus Christ.

On this side of the cross, we have clarity and God's Word empowered by the Holy Spirit to light our path and guide us into all righteousness. We have salvation, and with renewed purpose and a clear conscience, we believe they will be saved. In Romans 11, we see that "they have been blinded for our sake." (See Romans 11:25.) As commanded from scripture, we pray for the peace of Jerusalem and anticipate that many will come to faith. It is our collective prayer that God save the Jews! Sweet sisters, God is not finished with the Jews, and you are secure in God's love as well.

1. Read and record Romans 11:5 below.

2. Although the nation, Israel, had rejected Jesus, God remained faithful to save. Thousands of individual Jews came to faith. We must remember that God never loses sight of His eternal purposes. Record the last phrase of Acts 2:41 below, then answer, "Who is *'them'* "?

"Then those who gladly received his word were baptized;_____

_____" (Acts 2:41).

3. Thinking biblically, what is evidenced from Romans 11:5 and Acts 2:41 concerning election and God's gracious choice?

4. Did those who came to faith affect their salvation through any means, including works? Yes or no? _____. Please reference a verse in support of your answer.

5. A remnant remains. (See Romans 11:5.) The remnant was not called and chosen based on racial bias, worthiness, or good works, instead solely by God's grace. As you know, biblical grace is the unmerited, unearned favor of God. Let's examine "God's grace in the call" from both testaments. Complete the Old and New Testament verses below.

From the Old Testament: Deuteronomy 7:7-9

"The Lord did not set His _____ on you nor _____ you because you were more in number than any other people, for you were the _____ of all peoples; but because the Lord _____ you, and because He would keep the _____ which He swore to your fathers, the Lord has brought you out with a mighty hand, and _____ you from the house of bondage, from the hand of Pharaoh king of Egypt. 'Therefore know that the Lord your God, He *is* God, the _____ God who keeps _____ and _____ for a thousand generations with those who _____ Him and keep His _____;...' " (Deuteronomy 7:7-9).

From the New Testament: Ephesians 2:8-9

"For by _____ you have been _____ through _____ and that not of _____; *it is* the _____ of God, not of _____, lest anyone should boast" (Ephesians 2:8-9).

6. God makes a profound promise in Romans 11:26. In your own words, what does He pledge?

7. Does Romans 11:25 imply that all of Israel will come to faith? Please explain.

8. Read and review Isaiah 59:21. It is a covenant promise to Israel. How long does the Lord say that His spirit will be upon them and His Words in their mouths? Be specific.

9. God does not make mistakes nor change His mind. Concerning God's eternal choice, Israel will always be His covenant people. Romans 11:28 gives us a clue. What is revealed in Romans 11:28? From the verse, record God's partial explanation for Israel's coming salvation.

v. 28

10. Thinking biblically, who are the recorded *"fathers"* referenced in this verse? Hint: Those to whom the *"promise"* was given and passed generation after generation. They are sometimes identified as the patriarchs, which means any biblical figure regarded as "fathers of the human race." (i.e., the male head of the family or tribe.)

11. Read and review Exodus 2:24-25. These verses identify the patriarchs and record four noteworthy occurrences when the Israelites in bondage cried out to God from Egypt. Fill in the blanks from the appropriate passage.

a. God heard _____ and

b. God remembered _____

with _____

c. God looked _____

d. God acknowledged _____

♥ Heart-Check For Today

12. In faithfulness, God remembered His people! He will never forget the elect - all those predestined to be His in eternity. He will never lose sight of them, never turn a deaf ear towards them, or forsake His eternal promises to them. You may rest assured that when His purposes are fulfilled, the Jews will come to faith. **How merciful of God us set aside His people and provoke them to jealousy so that we might be saved?** (See Romans 11:11-15.)

With that thought in mind, prayerfully review Romans 11:29. In the space provided, record the first thoughts about God's electing call that comes to mind. Don't forget to include the date of your observation. Sometime in the future, you will be encouraged to discover what God has spoken to your heart through this rich promise on this very day. You are invited to share.

Romans 11:29 For the gifts and the calling of God are irrevocable.

Date:

My Thoughts on Romans 11:29:

Lesson 16: Restoration -
The Remnant Of Israel & Ingrafted Branches
Romans 11:1-36

Day Five: **Respond**. Review Romans 11:1-36

Memory Verse: "For the gifts and the calling of God are irrevocable" (Romans 11:29).

God remembered His promise! His call is irrevocable!

Sometimes we must go backward to move forward, and this is one of those times. To fully grasp the significance of God's infallible Word and unbroken promises, we must step back into the Old Testament to consider the depth of God's irrevocable call. Let's begin by tracing the Covenant that God remembered: "for the sake of their fathers." (See Romans 11:28.)

The Most High God is a promise keeper! He will never break a promise, and eventually, all that has been said by Him and about Him (in scripture) will come to pass. God's Word is true, and it is the standard by which all truth is judged. The mountains will melt like wax, but God's promises will endure! In due time, when God's work of salvation is complete, all the prophecies and covenant promises will be fulfilled. Do you know what God has promised and to whom?

To Abraham: Genesis 12:1-3, Genesis 15:1-21 and Genesis 17:1-22

To Isaac: God confirmed the promises with Isaac in Genesis 26:2-5

To Jacob: God confirmed the promises with Jacob in Genesis 28:10-15 and Genesis 35:9-15.

God made a unilateral covenant with Abraham and confirmed it with Isaac and later with Jacob. God ultimately planned that the entire world would be blessed through the "fathers of the faith" and their descendants. Additionally, God specifically promised land, a territory that could be identified geographically to the descendants of Abraham through Isaac and Jacob. God does not change His mind nor His plans. He planned to give them the land to possess it, root out the enemy, and bring glory and honor to His name. The Israelites were not only God's chosen, but His witnesses.

As the recipients of God's grace – that's His unfailing love, protection, and provision - and promise(s), they were to be His witness and testify of Him to a pagan world. Their peaceful presence, unwavering perseverance through adversity, and prevailing faith in the Great I AM were to contrast the enemies' travails in light of their man-made gods of wood and stone. The latter being earless, heartless, and lifeless. In stark contrast, Yahweh, the God of the patriarchs, heard the cries of His people and answered them from heaven! God's call was, and is, irrevocable, and His covenants are steadfast and true. What did God ask of them? The same thing He asks of us. God called them/us to faith in Him alone.

If you're unfamiliar with God's covenant promises, take some time to read through them. They will not only reveal God's plan and expose His love, but encourage your faith. To this very day, He has remembered His promises. Rejoice! Our living God is a faithful, promise-keeping God!

Let's review what He has said concerning the remembrance of the covenants for the sake of the fathers.

1. Read and review Exodus 2:24 and complete the passage.

"So God _____ their groaning, and God _____ His _____ with Abraham, with Isaac, and with Jacob" (Exodus 2:24).

2. Read and review Leviticus 26:42 and complete the passage.

"...then I will _____ My _____ with Jacob, and My _____ with Isaac and My _____ with _____ I will remember; I will remember the land" (Leviticus 26:42).

3. Read and review 2 Kings 13:23 and complete the passage.

"But the Lord was _____ to them, had _____ on them, and _____ them, because of His _____ with _____, _____, and _____, and would not yet _____ them or _____ them from His presence" (2 Kings 13:23).

4. The Jews did not continue in God's covenant as He had hoped. In apostasy and unbelief, many rejected Jesus, and as a consequence, God disregarded them. Romans 11 confirms that they were blinded for our sake and provoked to jealousy as we were grafted into the spiritual tree of Israel. The *"spiritual tree"* is made up of whoever believes in Jesus and calls upon His name. Therefore it pleased God to establish a New Covenant of grace by putting His laws "in their minds and writing it on their hearts." Let's take a closer look at Hebrews 8:6-12 to discover what God has said concerning His New Covenant on this side of the cross.

Read and review Hebrews 8:6-12 and complete the passages below.

v. 6 "But now He [Jesus] has obtained a more excellent ministry, inasmuch as He is also _____ of a _____ _____, which was established on better promises. v. 7 For if that first _____ had been _____, then no place would have been sought for a second."

v. 8 Because finding fault with them, He says: 'Behold, the days are coming, says the _____, when I will make a _____ _____ with the house of Israel and with the house of Judah v. 9 not according to the covenant that I made with their _____ in the day when I took them by the hand to lead them out of the land of Egypt; because they did not continue in My _____, and I _____ _____, says the Lord. v. 10 For this is the _____ that I will make with the house of _____ after those days, says the Lord: I will put My _____ in their _____ and write them on their _____; and **I will be their _____, and they shall be My _____**. (Emphasis added).

v. 11 None of them shall _____ his neighbor, and none his brother, saying, 'Know the Lord,' for _____ shall _____ _____, from the _____ of them to the _____ of them. v. 12 For I will be _____ to their _____, and their _____ and their _____ deeds **I will remember no more**" (Hebrews 8:6-12) (Emphasis added).

Review the verses above and complete the following questions.

5. In Hebrews 8:6, what was established on better promises?

6. In Hebrews 8:8, who did God find fault with?

Take note. Before Christ, our King-Priest, no priest ever sat down because their work was without end. Christ's work, however, was finished on Calvary. Consequently, He sat down! One Bible scholar said, "Christ is the best High Priest, who mediates the best covenant for us – the new covenant."

7. Review Hebrews 8:7-8. God references the flawed Old Covenant and makes a promise. Do you see God's mention of his flawed or insufficient covenant as well as God's promise? What did God promise because of the Old Covenant's incompleteness and imperfection?

8. After putting His laws in their minds and writing them on their hearts, what did God pledge from Hebrews 8:10? Be specific.

9. According to Hebrews 8:11, who shall know Him?

10. Read and record the last phrase of God's promise from Hebrews 8:12 below.

♥ <u>**Heart-Check For Today**</u>

11. God has promised you great things. Does His Word fill your heart and mind? If so, you are invited to share a testimony of God's faithful promises when you needed them most.

If God's promises aren't secure in your mind and written in your heart, what are you waiting on? His Word will remain forever. When the mountains melt like wax, His enduring Word will prevail. Moving forward, prayerfully ask God to:

    1.) Woo you into His Word.
    2.) Draw near as you practice His presence.
    3.) Fill your heart and mind with His rich promises.

Start slowly. Meditate on a few passages each day, and then commit them to memory. Nothing strengthens us for the journey better than feasting on God's Word. It's a healthy diet for the soul!

Here's one last thought about God's promises. It has been said, "Nothing encourages our faith more than recalling the rich promises of God." When our world unravels or a crisis comes, His promises keep us poised and steady. They not only secure us, but His Word equips us in every season of life. His Word prepares us to be His witness and bring honor and glory to His name. When His promises are secure in our minds and written in our hearts, we are prepared for whatever comes. God is forever faithful, as are His promises!

12. God demonstrated His faithfulness in the covenant to Abraham, then confirmed it to Isaac and, ultimately, to Jacob. Through the ages, He has shown that His promises are secure. Has God made a promise to you through scripture? I suspect that He has, for He is always speaking when we study His Word. Do you have a "go-to" verse that reveals God's faithfulness? If so, you are invited to share your top three verses in the order of their significance.

1.

2.

3.

Review your verses and prayerfully thank God for His faithfulness.

Words of Jesus
"Then Jesus cried out and said, 'He who believes in Me, believes not in Me but in Him who sent Me.'" (John 12:44).

Lesson 17: Living Sacrifices - Vessels Of Love
Romans 12:1-21

Day One: **Read**. Prayerfully Read Romans 12:1-21

Memory Verse: "And do not be conformed to this world, but be transformed by the renewing of your mind, that you may prove what is that good and acceptable and perfect will of God" (Romans 12:2).

Part II: The Redeemed and How We Behave - Romans 12-16

Romans Road Map: We begin Part II of our journey in Romans today. Paul's tone will change as he moves us into practical living for Christ in light of all we believe. He will beseech us to present our bodies as living sacrifices, holy, and acceptable to God. According to Paul, this is our reasonable service. (See Romans 12:1.) For believers, there is no other option.

Part I of our study (Romans chapters 1-11) united believers, both Jew and Gentile, under one God and Savior Jesus. It defined and identified what we believe and why we believe it! In the first eleven chapters, Paul systematically laid a secure foundation for our Christian faith. He began with an overview of man's depravity and hopelessness apart from Christ. It climaxed with every believer's hope in the glory of the resurrection. We owe our thanks to God! What began in despair ends in glory!

Among conservative Bible scholars, chapters 1-11 of Romans are considered the most doctrinally sound passages in the Bible. If you were wondering what we believe and why we believe it, Paul's inspired message has covered it all. No other book in the Bible outlines God's plan for humanity or the believer's call to faith in greater detail and more succinctly. Paul's epistle to the Romans has covered every essential aspect of our Christian faith.

As we turn our focus to the end of our journey, we can rejoice. As evidenced by Romans, we have a secure foundation, which is faith in Christ alone. Never doubt God's plan of salvation or His everlasting love for you. You are secure in Jesus! His love is without bounds; it is holy, pure, perfect - complete. You have been saved by grace through faith, and Jesus loves you just the way you are! Nothing can separate you from the love of God. (See Romans 8:38-39.)

As we move through Romans 12-16, we will put it all together. Many questions concerning righteous living will be answered. If you ever wondered what is the believer's response after faith comes, you're about to find out. Questions like: Are we duty-bound? What is our motivation? What do we hope to attain since we have already received the divine mercies due to us? Chapters 3 - 8 have highlighted the mercies of God's grace through our Lord Jesus in great detail. So that you know, mercy means that we receive God's grace rather than what we truly deserve. What more can He give? After all, He has given His life to give us life! We have salvation and right standing before God. Through Jesus, we are justified in the sight of God! In Him, we have forgiveness and eternal life. Our destiny has been changed. In short, we have victory now and forever! In Him, you have all you truly need.

The next move is ours. Therefore, how should we respond after faith comes? In light of the knowledge that God had called and chosen us with divine purpose and predestined us for greatness and all before the world began. What's that greatness? Simply stated, it's a place in His eternal kingdom where we shall reign with Him. So, again, what is our appropriate response? When we consider that we are joint-heirs with Christ to all that God can give, how, and from where do we respond?

We respond from the heart! It must come from a heart of love and devotion, not out of obligation or to earn God's favor. You already have God's favor – it's grace - His unearned, unmerited favor. You were saved by grace through faith. God favored you before you were ever born. You were chosen and called by God before the foundation of the world. God elected you to be a recipient of His amazing grace.

Therefore, our lives should be a living sacrifice worthy of all He has done. In Pauline fashion, he gets to the heart of the matter - our will and motives. Both will undergo a thorough examination as we journey through the remaining chapters of Romans. As living sacrifices, topics like how we love, how we serve, and all aspects of Godly submission, including our submission to the authorities placed over us, will be considered. And lastly, how do we, as believers, find unity in the love of

Christ? Christians are sometimes irritating or irregular people, but the blood of Jesus unites us to love all others after a pattern of Christ. Sometimes it's easier to love the nonbeliever because the mistakes and crises of their lives are to be expected. But when crises come to our brothers and sisters in Christ, loving them like Christ, sacrificially, and without judgment, through thick and thin, and to the bitter end, well, that's another matter! Needless to say, loving like Jesus is challenging.

So, how do we love all others in a way that pleases God? Paul will tell us. We do so in sacrifice. We imitate Jesus. Jesus has given Himself; He was the ultimate sacrifice. Now it's our turn. After faith comes, in love and devotion, we offer our lives back as a living sacrifice because, sweet sisters, it is our reasonable service! Open your Bibles to Romans 12, and let's get started.

Read Romans 12:1-8 and answer the following questions.

1. Paul beseeches you in Romans 12:1. By what?

2. Review Romans 12:1. As a living sacrifice, how were you to present your body?

3. From Romans 12:2, you were not to be conformed but transformed by what?

4. Review Romans 12:2. What would this prove?

5. Thinking biblically, how is the mind (your mind) renewed?

6. Thinking biblically, what is "the good and acceptable and perfect will of God"?

7. Read and review Romans 12:3. What is Paul's warning from this passage?

8. According to Romans 12:3, how has God dealt with you? And others?

9. Review Romans 12:4. Being many, what are we?

10. In your own words, describe what Romans 12:4 means.

11. Read and review Romans 12:6-8 and complete the passages.

"Having then _____ differing according to the _____ that is given to us, let us _____ them: if _____, let us prophesy in proportion to our _____; or _____, let _____ use it in our ministering; he who _____, in teaching; he who _____, in exhortation; he who _____, with liberality; he who _____, with diligence; he who shows _____, with _____" (Romans 12:6-8).

Lesson 17: Living Sacrifices - Vessels Of Love
Romans 12:1-21

Day Two: **Research**. Review Romans 12:1-21

Memory Verse: "And do not be conformed to this world, but be transformed by the renewing of your mind, that you may prove what is that good and acceptable and perfect will of God" (Romans 12:2).

I. Using a bible, bible dictionary, or concordance define the following **key words.**

beseech v. 1

conformed v. 2

transformed v. 2

hypocrisy v. 9

tribulation v. 12

hospitality v. 13

vengeance v. 19

II. Read the following **key phrases.**

a living sacrifice v. 1 - Jesus's death on the cross ended the Old Testament act of worship through sacrifice. On this side of the cross, the believer responds by becoming a "living sacrifice." It's our appropriate response of worship through sacrifice; it is our sacrificial worship. Watch this. Our response is not obligatory for cleansing or forgiveness of sins. Instead, it's in response to what God has accomplished through Christ's ultimate sacrifice on our behalf. Jesus' once and for all perfect and holy sacrifice satisfied the wrath of God, bringing to an end the Old Testament Temple sacrificial system.

The believer's "will" must be engaged to accomplish this act of worship. The picture in view is the believer placing their whole life on the altar as an act of worship in sacrificial service. Our lives should be consecrated to God. That means they are to be set apart, to God and for God. Namely, to surrender ourselves so that He might accomplish His perfect and pleasing will in and through the lives of those called and chosen - the redeemed - the family of God - His Church.

Since our "wills" govern our minds, we must reflect and recall this initial act of surrendering our bodies as "living sacrifices" every day. As Jesus' sacrifice was once and for all, ours is as well. However, we must daily reflect on this act of worship out of love and devotion to Jesus. Otherwise, our "wills," which govern our minds and guide our actions, words, and deeds, will not be engaged with God or for God's purposes. If you are married, you have pledged yourself to your spouse. Yielding to God every day is similar to recalling your pledge or marriage vows to your spouse and esteeming your spouse more significant than yourself. Have you not pledged your life and heart to Jesus? If so, you should recall it every day as an act of worship. If necessary, get a visual in the mind of your initial act of worship as a "living sacrifice" upon God's altar.

Concerning the believer's presentation of their bodies to God as a living sacrifice, one commentator said, *"That is what is acceptable to Him; that is what delights Him; that is what pleases Him; that is the appropriate response to Him and for Him."* In Romans 12:2, we see that Paul agrees. The implication here is that God expects our acceptable service (your yielded life as a sacrifice) because He has paid the ultimate sacrifice by accomplishing all we need through offering up His Son, Jesus.

Lastly, we imitate Christ through this act of worship. When we offer our bodies as a "living sacrifice," we identify with Christ's death on Calvary as only believers can. As we present our bodies as a "living sacrifice" (an acceptable act of worship), we do so for the benefit of the gospel. We do so in partnership with God to build up His Church and with eternity in view. Take notice of that statement.

That's not a new concept or one found only in Romans. Paul addressed the Church at Corinth with a similar message. Read 1 Corinthians 6:19-20 and complete the following.

"Or do you not know that _____ body is the _____ of the Holy Spirit *who is* in you, whom you have from God, and you are not your _____? For _____ were bought at a _____; therefore _____ God in your body and in your spirit, which are _____" (1 Corinthians 5:19-20).

We belong to God! Yielding our lives and glorifying God is not only reasonable; it is our supreme purpose. Lest we forget, the chief end of man is to glorify God and enjoy Him forever. As you present your body as a living sacrifice, you not only glorify God with your words, but your very body displays an attitude or posture of adoration and worship as well.

not lagging in diligence v. 11 - God wants to see a disciplined passion in His children. When God governs us, the fire and passion within us are tempered by Godly character, which is orderly and purposeful.

lagging - *From the Theological Dictionary of the New Testament,* lagging is *"hesitation through weariness, sloth, fear, bashfulness, or reserve. Lagging references hesitating, anxious, and negligent or slothful [lazy] behavior."* For clarity, let's explore other Bible translations of this phrase from Romans 12:11. They are as follows: King James Version (KJV), "not slothful in business;" from the English Standard Version (ESV), "Do not be slothful in zeal;" from the New Living Translation (NLT), "Never be lazy but work hard and serve the Lord."

The Theological Dictionary of the New Testament further states, "This sloth [lagging] is a serious matter because it ignores and neglects the responsibility <u>which the righteous must display</u> in the face of God's eternal judgment." (Emphasis added.) In Romans 12:11, Paul significantly relates the warning against sloth to the admonition to "be inspired and directed by the Spirit."

diligence - From the *Greek-English Lexicon of the New Testament,* "*to be eager to do something, with the implication of readiness to expend energy and effort—'to be eager, eagerness, devotion.'*"

Therefore, not lagging in diligence means do not hesitate, neglect, or slothfully approach what is good or right and noble or of high value, including any area of devotion or honorable acts of service. Believers should approach all they do with excellence, moral fortitude, and strength of character. Remember, we are Christ's representatives in all we do. We are admonished to do all things to the glory of God. Read and complete the last phrase of Colossians 3:17 below.

"And *whatever* you do in word or deed, *do* all in the name of the Lord Jesus, _____" (Colossians 3:17)

From the New Living Translation:

"And whatever you do or say, do it as a representative of the Lord Jesus, giving thanks through Him to God the Father" (Colossians 3:17).

fervent in spirit v. 11 - literally "to boil in spirit." The emphasis on this phrase is the "heat" to produce adequate, productive energy. That does not, however, suggest so much heat that we lack control in all matters. For reinforcement, read Acts 18:25.

patient in tribulation v. 12 - patience references the believer's endurance and ability to remain faithful even under tremendous trials, difficulty, or burdens. Things such as illness and disease, and persecution are in view. Mainly, Godly patience is required in all crises of life. He has given us His Spirit. Therefore, it's doable! The primary emphasis is on the believer's "endurance under pressure," which includes their forbearance, toleration, and acceptance of God's perfect and pleasing will for their lives, whatever that may entail.

live peaceably v. 18 - From the *Greek-English Lexicon of the New Testament*, *"to live in peace with others means 'to behave peacefully, to live in peace with one another.' In some languages, the equivalent of 'live in peace' is a negation of fighting, for example, 'do not fight' or 'do not constantly quarrel.' The basic meaning conveys the absence of war, the opposite of disturbance."*

Even though we cannot control others' thoughts, words, deeds, or actions, believers are admonished to live at peace with others - all others. Although we will encounter adversaries of the cross on this journey, we are to speak the truth in love and leave the results to God. We are called to take the "high road," which always leads to the cross. We are encouraged to esteem others more significant than ourselves and imitate the peaceful nature of Jesus. We do so through sacrificial love towards all others.

"If it is possible, as much as depends on you, live peaceably with all men" (Romans 12:18).

We are advised to live in peace with everyone, if possible. As His image-bearers, it's up to us to be peace-makers and not disrupters of peace instead.

Regarding *peace and our fellow workers of righteousness*, complete 1 Thessalonians 5:13:

"...and to esteem them _____ _____ in _____ for their work's sake. Be at _____ among yourselves."

vengeance is Mine v. 19 From the *Greek-English Lexicon of the New Testament - to repay harm with harm, on the assumption that the initial harm was unjustified and that retribution is therefore called for—'to pay back, to revenge, to seek retribution, retribution, seeking retribution.'"* Additionally, from the *Theological Dictionary of The New Testament (referencing Romans 12:19)* the referenced phrase does not mean, "do not procure justice for yourselves" but rather, "avenge not yourselves," for the divine judgment to which we yield replaces revenge.

It is not our call to judge or execute justice. The emphasis of implementing justice is based on the One who is just – God, our justifier - the only One able to execute divine and appropriate justice. Only God within Himself is just and fair. Justice is embedded within His character and nature - That's who God is!

Read Psalm 9:7-8. From verse 8, how with God judge the world?_____

Read Deuteronomy 32:4. This verse ascribes "the greatness of our God." List the five (5) God truths from the passage.

1._____

2._____

3._____

4._____

5._____

Lesson 17: Living Sacrifices - Vessels Of Love
Romans 12:1-21

Day Three: **Receive**. Review Romans 12:1-21

Memory Verse: "And do not be conformed to this world, but be transformed by the renewing of your mind, that you may prove what is that good and acceptable and perfect will of God" (Romans 12:2).

Believers are consecrated! The Bible assures it, even when we don't feel holy, sanctified, or dedicated to God, He declares it so. In other words, **we are set apart by God, to God, and for God.** Believer, your life is not your own; the blood of Jesus ransomed it. Pause for a moment to consider the encouraging words of Peter and Paul from 1 Peter 2:9-10 and Romans 12:1-2, respectively. As you can see, in the spiritual sense, it's accomplished. But how does it translate in the natural? And what is our part?

Collectively, Christ's Church has a responsibility to demonstrate a God-honoring, Christ-centered lifestyle. That is always counter-cultural. As individual believers, our lives should express His love and forgiveness. Always, it should be apparent to everyone that we are different and unique, for we are hidden with Christ in God. We have Christ in us, the hope of glory, and that truth should prevail in our lives and be seen by everyone. We should display His love and tender mercies every day, and that begins at home. That has always been part of God's plan for His people. We should exalt Him and bring honor and glory to His name in all things at all times. Even and most expressly, in the presence of the enemy.

When Abraham built an altar, worshiped, and praised God, it was in the presence of the enemy. Pagans were in the land! No doubt, his bold actions challenged the culture of that day, riveting them to their cores. (See Genesis 12.) In essence, Abraham's worshipful lifestyle said, "My God rules and reigns and I will worship Him, I will follow Him, and I will serve Him and Him alone. I belong to Him! He is my God, and I am His people."

One commentator suggested concerning Romans 12, "Jesus is either Lord of all or not at all." Is He Lord of your life? Do you think about Jesus? Is He ruling and reigning within you? If so, are you yielding to His spirit? Are you being transformed into His image rather than conformed to the world around you? Psalm 107:2 admonishes, "Let the redeemed of the Lord say so…" Put that confession into action. If you are His, you must gladly demonstrate it in a sacrificial lifestyle of love that pushes against the culture of today and exalts our one true Lord, who is Lord of all!

Believers are called to love! Because Christ has loved us and deposited His love in us, we are called to love – everyone. Indeed, within that group, we must love other believers in a way that honors Jesus. There is no room for conceit, deceit, or self-exaltation among the members of Christ's body. Your gifts have been mercifully given and promote an eternal purpose - namely salvation. That means they're never for self-promotion or earthly gain. Likewise, they should not lead to popularity or riches. Instead, Christ has distributed them with forethought before the world's formation to exalt Himself and advance His kingdom. Therefore, these gifts not only glorify Him, but they're also an expression of His boundless love and have eternity in view.

Unveiling Love.

In Romans 12, Paul begins by unveiling love. He challenges us to live a life that places Christ's love to everyone above all else. If we don't live for Christ and love like Christ, who shall do it? We are His only vessels for good, truth, and love upon the earth. Hope comes, faith comes, and ultimately salvation comes through love and goodness, not through harsh judgment, criticism, and never vengeance. Vengeance belongs to Him alone. (See Romans 12:19.) Was it not His unfathomable love and mercy that first captivated your heart? Did God not love you into His kingdom? Yes, of course, He did!

Church, we are His hands and feet. We are salt and light. We are a divine force for love, hope, and eternal life against a hostile culture in a dying world. We are called to demonstrate Christ's love in faithfulness because that's God's plan. If you're saved, you're called to be His witness. (See Acts 1:8.)

What's at stake if we don't live for Christ and look like Christ? Tragically, the gospel. That's why we must love sacrificially, esteeming all others as more significant than ourselves. As we love after a pattern of Christ, we declare to those perishing around us that our God lives and reigns. Our lives testify "God is alive," and is waiting to save "whoever calls upon the name of the Lord" (Romans 10:13).

Paul's message will challenge and inspire you. As you receive God's word into your heart, take the time for self-examination. Paul's exhortations seem so simple on the surface, but apart from the empowerment of the His Holy Spirit, which is "at home" in you, it is impossible. Remember, real and lasting change comes from within and is empowered by His spirit. I urge you to yield fully with love and joy.

1. Review Romans 12:9. Paul gives three instructions in this passage. List them below.

    a._____

    b._____

    c._____

2. From Romans 12:10, what is the clue to brotherly love? Be specific.

3. Paul makes 8 key points to guide loving relationships in Romans 12:11-13. Please record them below.

    a._____

    b._____

    c._____

    d._____

    e._____

    f._____

g._____

h._____

4. We all experience some measure of persecution in this life. Paul shared with Timothy in 2 Timothy 3:12, "In fact, everyone who wants to live a Godly life in Christ Jesus will be persecuted." Record Romans 12:14 below. Herein, Paul gives us wisdom concerning persecution.

Romans 12:14 –

5. Thinking biblically, why would Paul give such instruction? What would be the benefit? If possible, record a scripture in support of your thoughts.

6. Paul addresses believers and their love and service toward other believers in Romans 12:14-21. For the most part, these instructions are echoed by Paul in other epistles. Paul's concern is how we exhibit Godly love for one another through more than *"mere words."* Our attitudes, motivation, and daily dealings with one another should reflect Christ's love. After all, His spirit resides in us. Paul knew as we do, relationships can be complicated, but great wisdom is found within this exhortation. Jesus said, "they will know you by your love." (See John 13:35.) This love, which Jesus referenced, reflects His nature and character. It is kind and gentle, compassionate, sacrificial, and has no other motivation but esteeming others' needs greater than its own.

Prayerfully read and review Romans 12:14-21. What specific instruction is contained within these verses? Lessons Four and Five will provide a thorough examination of Paul's teachings. Complete each thought below. Be specific.

a. Concerning persecution:_____

b. Concerning rejoicing:_____

c. Concerning weeping:_____

d. Concerning the mind:_____

e. Concerning humility:_____

f. Concerning your opinion:_____

g. Concerning evil:_____

h. Concerning your regard:_____

i. Concerning peaceable living:_____

j. Concerning vengeance:_____

7. Paul wraps up his exhortation by quoting the wisdom of Solomon from Proverbs 25:21-22.

Record Romans 12:20 below.

Romans 12:20 -

8. How do we combat evil in a way that honors Jesus? Romans 12:21 captures His heart on the matter and instructs us -

not to:_____

but to:_____

9. When you think about overcoming evil, does love come to mind? Can you recall a time when love prevailed, and it transformed a crisis into a miracle from God? If so, please share your testimony. Remember, our testimony must be shared; it encourages others on the journey and exalts Jesus. It is your opportunity as the redeemed "to say so....!" Remember John's inspired message from Revelation 12:11, "And they overcame him [Satan] by the blood of the Lamb and by the word of their testimony..."

Maybe you recall a time when you failed in the area of love? It happens. At times we miss what God is trying to accomplish through us. Don't despair; He will give you another opportunity to love sacrificially and achieve His purposes. Who does God use? Anyone He chooses! He will use you as you yield to Him, practice His presence, and praise and worship Him in sight of the enemy! Your next opportunity is right around the corner. Pray for divine encounters and a chance to share His sacrificial love. He always answers these prayers in the affirmative.

♥ Heart-Check For Today

10. Do you feel unloving? Are you struggling to love someone in a way that honors Jesus? If so, take it to Him in prayer. As you receive Paul's words about love into your heart, rejoice - Jesus is faithful. He is love, and He will give you as much love as you can handle. If you need encouragement or special prayer in this area, ask your leader or pastor. Be honest. Remember, we can't give what we've not received. Out of prayer, from meditating on His Word, and from fellowship with Jesus, love grows. The more time you spend in His Word and at His feet, the more love you will have. You're invited to close in prayer.

Lesson 17: Living Sacrifices - Vessels Of Love
Romans 12:1-21

Day Four: **Reflect**. Prayerfully Review Romans 12:1-21

Memory Verse: "And do not be conformed to this world, but be transformed by the renewing of your mind, that you may prove what is that good and acceptable and perfect will of God" (Romans 12:2).

As we reflect on what God has said through Paul's epistle to the Romans, the focus of today's lesson will be Romans 12:9-13. What would God have us to remember concerning **faith that produces love** in the heart of His church?

Read and review Romans 12:9. Paul says our love should be without hypocrisy. It's to be sincere, not imitating or masquerading as love, but rather, a genuine and authentic love. From the *Theological Dictionary of the New Testament*, "'*hypocrisy or the feigning of love' conflicts with the truth and clarity of God from which the acts and attitudes of Christians proceed.*'" In Paul's letter to Timothy, he concluded that "love is the heart of the Christian message." Simply stated, Paul said that love is the fruit of pure belief, and it comes from genuine faith. Love is the basis of Christianity.

1. In Romans 12:9, we see a contrast between good and evil.

   a. From Romans 12:9, what does Paul advise concerning good? Concerning evil?

   b. Thinking biblically, what does Paul's advice concerning evil mean?

2. Referencing Romans 12:9, we find from the *Theological Dictionary of the New Testament* that "*'evil' refers very generally to what is morally bad.*" Paul has clearly shown us the opposite in revealing what "is good" in Romans 12:2. Read and review Romans 12:2. As a result of spiritual transformation and the renewing of our minds, we are to ***prove*** something in Romans 12:2 and ***cling*** to something in Romans 12:9.

We are to prove:_____

We are to cling:_____

3. Review Romans 12:2 again. What three words describe the "will of God?"

_____   _____   _____

4. In the very next verse, Romans 12:3, Paul moves to the topic of love. Not just love, rather "brotherly love." All love comes from God. In essence, He is the embodiment of love. We cannot know love or express love apart from God's love. If you love God, you will loathe or hate what is evil and regard it with horror. Tragically, in light of political correctness, we have become desensitized. The global church struggles to call out sin, as sin, and evil, as evil. One theologian stated concerning the evil of our times, "Unfortunately, familiarity with a culture that is shaped by the forces of Satan has lulled too many believers into a state of general tolerance for whatever deviant behavior is in vogue at present. As believers, we are to detest or loathe evil because it is the enemy of all that leads to Christlikeness."

Sin not only leads to destruction and painful consequences, but it also separates us from fellowship with God. Nonetheless, we live in a fallen world, and corruption abounds. Evil's presence is unavoidable. So, what can we do? Follow Abraham's lead. We can be God's witness at all times and in all places.

With that thought in mind, when was the last time you were confronted with evil and neglected the opportunity to call it out? What stopped you? If you get a do-over, how might you respond?

5. Abhorring evil and clinging to what is good in Romans 12:9 links us to Romans 12:2. What instruction is recorded in the verse that leads to proving what is "*that good, perfect and pleasing will of God?*" For your answer, record the first two phrases of verse 2 below.

6. According to Paul, how should you renew your mind?

7. Read and review Romans 12:10. Then, in a sentence or two, define brotherly love.

8. In Romans 12:10, Paul says we are to give preference to one another. He has made this appeal to the Philippians as well. What instruction has Paul given concerning an expression of brotherly love from Philippians 2:3? Complete the verse below.

"Let nothing be done through selfish _____ or _____, but in _____ of mind let _____ esteem _____ than _____" (Philippians 2:3).

9. The members of our family now extend beyond the four walls called home. Paul has broadened the scope of our responsibility in *"brotherly love and kindly affection."* Who are your brothers and sisters, and how are we related?

Our brotherly love and warm affection are empowered by the Holy Spirit, which is "at home" in us. Infused with the Spirit of God, we have a new life – it's Christ in us! Our outlook and attitudes have a new point of reference - the indwelling Spirit of God. (See Romans 8:9; 11.) That's not a new concept; Paul has shared this truth before. He also informed the Church at Colossi in Colossians 1:27, referencing the great mystery of God's Church, that they had Christ in them, and as a result, the hope of eternal life. God picks us and, then, embodies us. As a result, we have Christ in us, our hope of glory. It's interesting to note, too, that we have no say in whom God chooses. It's all up to Him. Salvation is His work, He's building His church, and it's made up of those He chose and called before the foundation of the world. Thankfully, we are a diverse group, coming from all nations, from all walks of life, and possessing much cultural diversity. Many are poor, while others are rich. Some members are young, while others are old. Yet, in Christ, we are united, we have one heart and mind (spiritually), for we have Christ in us, and He alone is our hope of glory.

Believers are a peculiar lot, indeed. As a result, among us, we will encounter annoying, irritating, and irregular people. Perhaps you know some or are one yourself. Regardless, by God's divine choice, we are one united in Christ. From his book, *Roots of Righteousness,* noted pastor and Bible scholar A. W. Tozer stated, *"A real Christian is an odd number anyway. He feels supreme love for One whom he has never seen, talks familiarly every day to "Someone" he cannot see, expects to go to heaven on the virtue of "Another," empties himself in order to be full, admits he is wrong so he can be declared right, goes down in order to get up, is strong when he is weakest, is richest when he is poorest, and happiest when he feels worst. He dies so he can live, forsakes in order to have, gives away so he can keep, sees the invisible, hears the inaudible, and knows that which passes knowledge."*

As both Paul and Dr. Tozer describe, a Christ-centered, Christ-honoring life is focused on eternal things - God's kingdom and winning souls to fill it. The words in Romans 12:11-13 characterize such a life, a life indwelled by Christ that is at liberty to love all others because they have experienced God and His unfailing love. Complete the passage from Romans 12:11-13 below.

"...not lagging in _____ fervent in _____ _____ the Lord; _____ in hope, _____ in tribulation, continuing _____ in prayer; distributing to the _____ of the saints, given to _____" (Romans 12:11-13).

10. Reflect on Romans 12:11-13 and consider the following. How are you doing in the area of brotherly love and kindly affection?

    Am I esteeming others greater than myself?

    Am I diligent in all things?

    Am I fervent in spirit? (That means you're being stirred or moved by the Holy Spirit to show great eagerness towards something of eternal and lasting value. It demonstrates your kingdom vision and purpose in doing God's work God's way.)

    Am I serving the Lord?

    Am I rejoicing in hope?

    Am I patient in tribulation?

    Am I continuing steadfastly in prayer?

    Am I hospitable?

    Am I given to the needs of the saints?

So, we consider this. "What would God have us to remember concerning **faith that produces love** in the heart of His church? We can begin by remembering these important basics.

First – Remembering that by faith, the Christian life is a life of love, sacrifice, and devotion. According to Paul, our kindly affection and brotherly love are expressed through our devotion, service, hospitality, and prayers for its members. It is also conveyed in meeting the needs of others and rejoicing in hope, and remaining patient in tribulation. This expression of brotherly love begins in our immediate family, and then it extends to our family of faith - Christ's church. The point here is that God's love, which has been freely given and received - pours into us to overflowing - and then naturally flows outward for the benefit of others.

In brotherly love, we must lay our personal feelings and agendas aside. Among us, there is no room for personal preference or discrimination; our likes and dislikes become irrelevant. The church should never become a house of cliques where Christian charity and harmony are extended only to those of our choosing. We don't decide who is worthy of brotherly love. God has already decided. He's chosen His family (His church) and multiplies it daily, according to His divine will and purpose. That warrants repeating and leads us to our second point.

Second – Remembering that God builds the house and calls its members. It's not your job! He has intentionally handpicked each of its members, including you, with divine purpose from eternity past. Nor is it your job to withhold God's love from others, especially your spiritual family. Remember this. When we love like Jesus, we look like Jesus, and that's what attracts the lost. We imitate Jesus when we express His love and generosity without debate, criticism, or judgment. Lest we forget, we will be responsible for our performance in loving one another. Through Paul, God's Word has called us into account.

Third – and lastly, remembering that within God's family, brotherly love and kindly affection are crucial. If we don't get it right there, we will never get it right beyond church walls. What's at stake? As always, the gospel! But rest assured! In Jesus, we have all we need. God has poured His love into us! **Therefore, our devoted service unto God is: birthed in His love, identified with His love, influenced by His love, and empowered by His love. Most clearly, our devoted service to others is an extension of God's love.**

11. Let's conclude by looking at four critical passages. As you allow God's Word to wash over you, consider your call to brotherly love or loving like Christ!

"But concerning brotherly love you have no need that I should write to you, for you yourselves are taught by God to love one another;..." (1 Thessalonians 4:9)

What was Paul's message from 1 Thessalonians 4:9?

Paul also spoke to the Galatians about love and service to the family of faith, saying:

"Therefore, as we have opportunity, let us do good to all, especially to those who are of the household of faith" (Galatians 6:10).

Sweet sisters, we will be known. Others will see us and identify us, as God's elect or not. For our life is our testimony, and it writes a story every day. Jesus said it like this:

"By this all will know that you are My disciples, if you have love for one another" (John 13:35).

That's more than a mere suggestion; we are commanded to love. It is our first responsibility as believers. When Jesus was asked, what is the greatest commandment, this was His response.

"And you shall love the Lord your God with all your heart, with all your soul, with all your mind, and with all your strength. This is the first commandment. And the second, like it, is this: 'You shall love your neighbor as yourself.' There is no other commandment greater than these" (Mark 12:30-31).

Take note. The word *"love"* from Mark 12:31 is a command in the original Greek. Jesus said, "There is no other commandment greater than these." It appears that we have no choice as children of God; it's our call. Once again, when we fail to love others in the manner that God desires, the gospel is at stake.

It's been said that our genuine love for people is an expression of our sincere love for God. We must make it personal, and here's the litmus test. If you genuinely love God, you will love people. That's the bottom line. It's doable, with His Spirit's help. Remember, loving in that way not only blesses the heart of God, but it sets us apart from all others. To that end, may God's love and grace fill you to overflowing. Then, may you serve Him fearlessly as you love others into the Kingdom.

As you conclude, reflect on God's love for you. Ask Him to empower you to love others in a way that honors Him. He will surely do it. You are invited to close in prayer.

Lesson 17: Living Sacrifices - Vessels Of Love
Romans 12:1-21

Day Five: **Respond**. Review Romans 12:1-21

Memory Verse: "And do not be conformed to this world, but be transformed by the renewing of your mind, that you may prove what is that good and acceptable and perfect will of God" (Romans 12:2).

Yesterday's lesson was framed by a question, "What would God have us to remember concerning **faith that produces love** in the heart of His church?" Keep this question in mind as we bring our study of Romans 12 to a close.

As you ponder that question, let's break it down. "What makes for a loving church? What's the formula?" As you shall see, a faith that produces love in our hearts is activated or realized through prayer. That's the only way, and if prayer is neglected, we are unloving. Subsequently, this affects the church because guess what? The global church – Christ's Church – is comprised of believers, just like us, who are either loving or not. We are His church. Lest we forget, we are the face of Jesus to a perishing world. We are His arms and feet, too, as well as His purveyors of love, hope, and peace on the earth.

So, let's begin today's study by taking an honest and biblical look at prayer. First, prayer is perhaps the most misunderstood weapon at the believer's disposal. Why? Because, generally speaking, it's not only misunderstood, but it's also under-used and under-valued. That's tragic because, through prayer, we have direct access to God. That means that we can enjoy immediate access with Our Creator every moment of every day. Second, prayer is a spiritual barometer of sorts. It reveals the measure of our faith, as well as what fills our hearts. Third, it demonstrates our need for God and fellowship with Him. Therefore, when we pray, how we pray and our desire to pray tells us a lot about our relationship with Jesus. Ideally, we want to spend time with those we love, and if you're going to spend time with Jesus, prayer is how it happens.

Pause for a minute and consider your prayer life. How often do you pray? Paul recommended "continuing steadfastly in prayer." (See Romans 12:12.) His recommendation speaks to our faithful service in prayer because it is the greatest weapon in our arsenal. It's also a Godly discipline, and we're commanded to pray. Be honest. If you were heading into battle, would you go unequipped? Of course not! You would engage every weapon you could avail to arm and equip yourself for war. We must remember, we're in a battle; we are soldiers in the army of God.

Prayer is our lifeline to the Father and Jesus. It's where we report for duty and receive our assignment. It's also where we are fortified and come into agreement with God (His Word). Prayer is where our hearts are tenderized, and love is birthed. It is the spiritual discipline that purifies our hearts and minds. It's where we unburden our souls, are cleansed and forgiven, and pick up the mantel which God has prepared for us. Consequently, for the believer, a faithful and productive prayer life is not only essential and desirable – it's everything!

1. The disciples got it. How so? They never asked Jesus to teach them to fish, to heal, to resurrect the dead, or to walk on water, but they did ask of Jesus, "Lord, teach us to pray." Luke addresses this very issue. Luke 11:1 exposes the disciple's collective hearts as well as their lack of understanding concerning prayer. Although they knew it was a crucial part of Jesus' life, they lacked sufficient knowledge to engage therein effectively. So, they asked the Lord to help them. Read and record their request below.

Luke 11:1

Likewise, we should follow the disciples' lead. If you are lacking or feel ineffective in prayer, ask Jesus to help you. He will most assuredly come to your aid.

2. Jesus was devoted to prayer because He knew the source of His strength. Moreover, He lived to accomplish God's express will and purposes, which were determined before the foundation of the world. Jesus knew He could not accomplish this in His strength, yet He never lost sight of His goal. Over and over again, we see Jesus turn to His Father in prayer. There He received God's wisdom and guidance, as well as strength. Read Jesus' words from John 6:38. What did Jesus confess about His earthly ministry? Be specific.

How, when, and where did Jesus pray? Let's take a look. Scripture is not void of examples of Jesus' devout prayer life. He was always in prayer. That means Jesus had a heart of prayer and an attitude, posture, and disposition of prayer.

Generally speaking, Jesus' prayers were much like ours in that some were public, and some were private. Unlike most of us, however, He was devoted to prayer - Jesus truly prayed without ceasing! He often neglected sleep finding refreshing, instead, in an all-night conversation with His Father. Before making any critical decisions, before moving forward, before and after healing, and when seeking and discerning His Father's will, Jesus prayed. He spoke on the importance of prayer and modeled it by allowing others to see Him turn to the Father in prayer.

Moreover, He taught the disciples to pray and gave them (and us) the Lord's Prayer as our model. Passionately and prostrate before God, Jesus prayed before He went to the cross. He prayed about the cross, about us, and on our behalf as well. His high priestly prayer is found in John 17. This treasury of scripture reveals much about His immense love, not only for us but for His Father as well. What more can we say? Jesus prayed, even from the cross – He prayed! His devoted life of prayer deserves a closer look. Although the following list is not exhaustive, it exposes Jesus' passionate and devout prayer life.)

In the gospels, Jesus prayed:

- at His baptism; before traveling from place to place
- before and after healing the sick; all night before choosing His disciples
- before and while speaking to Jewish leaders
- before feeding the 5,000 and well as the 4,000
- before Peter identified Him (Jesus) as – "the Christ"
- at the Transfiguration; at the return of the 70;
- before teaching His disciples to pray
- before raising Lazarus from the dead; before the laying on of His hands
- before caressing the little children and bidding them come;
- when asking the Father to glorify His Name
- for Peter, before He allowed Satan to sift him like wheat
- at the Lord's Supper; at the institution of what we know as Communion
- in intercession – in John 17, praying for Himself, for His disciples, and all believers
- for His church

- in Gethsemane three times, including the most impassioned Words of His life, Jesus prayed. "Your will be done."

From the Cross, Jesus prayed:

- on behalf of His assailants and accusers - begging God's merciful forgiveness
- before He died, He prayed that His Father had not forgotten Him
- in His dying breath, He ended His earthly life and ministry with this final prayer, "Father into thy hands, I commit my spirit."

After His resurrection, Jesus continued to pray

- blessing of the bread; before He ate, and with others
- in the presence of His disciple; before His Ascension

After His Ascension, Jesus continues to pray:

- at the right hand of the Father, Jesus is interceding for us

As you can see, Jesus was a devout man of prayer!

Prayer activated and unleashed God's power. Jesus was linked to God the Father, the great I AM all the days of His earthly life. He has left us a marvelous example of praying without ceasing. We should follow His example and endeavor to pray without ceasing.

Do you lack wisdom, patience, love, understanding, courage, humility, peace, satisfaction, or sufficient faith? Do you need healing or strength in your mind, body, or spirit? Then follow His lead - pray to your heavenly Father – ask Him! He is waiting to hear from you and answer your prayers.

♥ Heart-Check For Today

3. Prayerfully consider the following questions.

    a. Do I understand the importance of prayer?

    b. Am I prayerfully seeking God's will for my life?

    c. Am I giving thanks in all things in prayer?

4. Review the Lord's Prayer in Matthew 6:9-13. It is our perfect model for prayer. When our time for prayer is short, when matters of the day press heavy on our hearts, or when we don't know what to pray, we can turn to this perfect prayer. These words align us with God. But more than that, they remind us who God is, the Creator, in light of who we are, His creation. These words bring Godly order to all our concerns, for they allow us to worship, praise, and affirm our faith in the God in whom we have believed.

5. Read and review Romans 12:14-16. Some of these exhortations are in a positive form, and others take on a negative state. Examine the exhortation(s) or appeals from each verse and identify whether it is a negative or positive admonition. Complete the chart below with your findings.

	Positive	Negative
v. 14		
v. 15		
v. 16		

To fully grasp God's instruction through the inspired words of Paul, we must look to the original language. Consider each words' original meaning from the *Greek-English Lexicon of the New Testament.* After you review the definitions, answer question #6, which follows.

"**bless** - to ask God to bestow divine favor on, with the implication that the verbal act itself constitutes a significant benefit—'to bless, blessing.' "

"**rejoice** - to enjoy a state of happiness and well-being—'to rejoice, to be glad.' "

"**persecute** - In a number of languages, the equivalent of to 'persecute' is simply 'to cause to suffer,' but persecution is also expressed in terms of 'to be mean to' or 'to threaten' or 'to chase from place to place.' "

"**curse** - to cause injury or harm by means of a statement regarded as having some supernatural power, often because a deity or supernatural force has been evoked—'to curse, curse.' "

"**humble** - pertaining to having low and humble status—'lowly, humble; from the root of **humility** which is the state of low status, with the implication of humility—'low status, low estate, humility.' Additionally, from the *Theological Dictionary of the New Testament*, we find humble defined as 'unpretentious,' which means not attempting to impress others with an appearance of greater importance, talent, or culture than is actually possessed."

"**opinion** - a view or judgment not necessarily based on fact or knowledge; coming from within oneself. A matter of opinion is not generally capable of being proven either way. The origin of the word is English via Old French from Latin *opinio(n-)* from the stem *opinari* meaning 'to think, believe.' "

By in large, our opinions are formed, shaped, and influenced by various sources. Our upbringing, relationships, culture, the enemy, prevailing sin, and the world around us also weigh in. Therefore, the word of caution from this verse would be to check the source of our opinion. Always start with this question. Is it (my opinion) conformed to God's view on the matter? Only His opinion will carry the desired weight. If your opinion, on any matter, is aligned with God's, you are on the right track. If not, keep it to yourself because pride in the heart always demands the last word. God's Word must be our preeminent source on every matter.

6. Prayerfully review the definitions above. Do you struggle in any of these areas presently? Are you struggling with humility? Are you over-opinionated, insistent upon having the last word? Are you blessing those who persecute you? Can you feel the sorrow of others and passionately weep with them? Can you rejoice in the success of others without succumbing to bitterness or envy? Be honest. You are invited to share your thoughts and concerns. Please include in your testimony your path to success in accomplishing these exhortations from Paul.

Today's date:

Today, I am struggling in this area(s)

By God's grace and for His glory, this is my plan moving forward:

7. Paul concludes his exhortations with the following passage. Please complete the words from Romans 12:17-19.

"Repay no one _____ for _____. Have regard for _____ things in the sight of all _____. If it is possible, as much as depends on you,_____ _____ with all men. Beloved, do not _____ yourselves, but *rather* give place to wrath; for it is written, '_____ is _____, *I will* _____,' says the Lord."

8. We never pay back evil for evil. Paul conveys the heart of God in this instruction. God is love, and vengeance belongs to Him alone. Only He is worthy of judging and punishing evil. Who are we to repay evil when we are recipients of His divine mercy, which means we have His favor rather than what we have truly deserved.

"See that no one renders _____ for _____ to anyone, but always pursue what is _____ both for _____ and for _____" (1 Thessalonians 5:15).

9. As believers, we must respect what is good (or right) and honor God in our efforts. We are called to live peaceably with all men, for this exalts our Father in heaven. Are you living peaceably with others? If not, pray that God changes your heart. You can't bring about change in anyone but yourself. But, with God's help, you can have victory over this struggle as you surrender your will to Him. It is a marvelous thing to forgive. Nothing heals the humbled heart faster than remembering all that you have been forgiven.

10. God will have the final say. One day soon, all evil will be justly handled. God will execute His judgment for He promises,

"Vengeance is Mine, and recompense; Their foot shall slip in due time; For the day of their calamity is at hand, And the things to come hasten upon them" (Deuteronomy 32:35).

Let God be God in this situation. Then, pray for those over whom you would like to exact judgment and vengeance. We must love and pray for our enemies. (See Matthew 5:44.) We must leave God's perfect work to Him. The world would be a better and safer place if we trusted all things into His loving care. Are you willing to trust God and allow Him to avenge all things according to His mercy? Has He not been merciful to you? Your space for response is below.

"Because God has been merciful toward me and I'm forgiven all things, I will forgive _____." (insert the name(s) here).

Don't hold back. Purify your heart, forgive your enemy(s) and leave the results to God!

11. As we close today's lesson, Paul's final words from Romans 12:21 were, "Do not be overcome by evil, but overcome evil with good." Thinking biblically, how might you partner with God to overcome evil with good?

12. We are in a battle. Are you dressed for it? Prayerfully review Ephesians 6:14-18 and complete the partial phrases. The best-dressed believer wears the full armor of God.

v. 14 - stands firm with the belt of _____; with the_____ of righteousness;

v. 15 - with feet fitted with preparation that comes from the _____ of peace;

v. 16 - takes up the shield of _____;

v. 17 - takes the _____ of _____ and the sword of the _____. which is the word of God.

v. 18 He _____ in the Spirit...praying for all the Lord's people.

Words From Jesus
" 'And you shall love the Lord your God with all your heart, with all your soul, with all your mind, and with all your strength.' This is the first commandment. And the second, like it, is this: 'You shall love your neighbor as yourself.' There is no other commandment greater than these" Mark 12:30-31).

Lesson 18: Submission To Authorities & Loving Like Christ
Romans 13:1-14

Day One: **Read**. Prayerfully Read Romans 13:1-14

Memory Verse: "...and if there is any other commandment, are all summed up in this saying, namely, 'You shall love your neighbor as yourself.' Love does no harm to a neighbor; therefore love is the fulfillment of the law" (Romans 13:9(a)-10).

Prayerfully review Romans 13:1-7 and complete the following.

1. From Romans 13:1, who is to be subject to the governing authorities? Be specific.

2. According to Paul, leaders are divinely appointed, and all believers have a responsibility to them. Again, review Romans 13:1 and list everything that is said about authority.

3. From verse 13:2, what specific things are stated concerning those who resist authority?

4. According to Romans 13:3, rulers are not a terror to _____ _____, but to_____.

5. From Romans 13:3, we see it is possible to be "*unafraid*" of those governing at God's request. What are Paul's instructions to eliminate fear? Be specific.

6. According to the first phrase of Romans 13:3, who is God's minister, and what is his primary purpose?

7. Review Romans 13:4. If the believer does evil, what should he be? _____

8. From Romans 13:4, who does not bear the sword in vain? _____

9. From Romans 13:4, how is the work of God's minister described? Be specific. Record the last phrase of verse 4 for your answer.

10. Thinking biblically, what does it mean to practice evil? Can you give a specific example of evil?

11. Generally speaking, what is the source of all evil? Please record a scripture in support of your answer.

12. Review Romans 13:5. What must we be for conscience's sake?

13. From Romans 13:6, what does Paul instruct concerning taxes, and for what purpose? Be specific.

14. In Romans 13:7, Paul lists four things that should be rendered to the appropriate authorities. Record the verse below, underlining the four things that should be rendered.

Romans 13:7 -

Lesson 18: Submission To Authorities & Loving Like Christ
Romans 13:1-14

Day Two: **Research**. Review Romans 13:1-14

Memory Verse: "...and if there is any other commandment, are all summed up in this saying, namely, 'You shall love your neighbor as yourself.' Love does no harm to a neighbor; therefore love is the fulfillment of the law" (Romans 13:9(a)-10).

I. Using a bible, bible dictionary, or concordance define the following *key words.*

authority; authorities v. 1, 2, 3 -

ordinance v. 2 -

avenger v. 4 -

render v. 7 -

adultery v. 9 -

covet v. 9 -

revelry v. 13 -

II. Read the following *key phrases.*

Governing authorities v.1- From the *Theological Dictionary of the New Testament,* we read the following. *" 'Governing' generally defines the authorities as those who bear rule. The Greek-English Lexicon of the New Testament says it like this. " 'Governing authorities' exercise continuous control over someone or something -'to control, to restrain.' " Referencing Paul's day, o*ne commentator suggested that most of those "governing authorities" were nonbelievers. <u>If that be the case, they governed from a worldly point of reference, apart from the knowledge of God,</u> but by His divine appointment. (Emphasis added.)

Nonetheless, Paul says, "You [believers] are subject to them [governing authorities]." Therefore, the emphasis on Paul's instruction is that believers must remember those placed in these positions were raised up, confirmed, and established by God. God, alone, is the sole source of authority. Look at those who are governing you. Like it or not, it has pleased God to delegate authority to those in charge of every aspect of the public's well-being. He does so with purpose and for reasons that we don't understand. Who can know the mind of God? His primary focus, however, is always "our good." Take note. He has not established governing authorities as a means of punishment, instead to avoid disorder and violence, because the absence of law and order always breeds chaos or anarchy. We all need boundaries for our good and the betterment of society as a whole. Without debate, Paul affirms, "God has established the authorities that exist." (See Romans 13:1.)

Peter echoes Paul's thoughts on governing authorities. Complete 1 Peter 2:13-14 below.

"Therefore _____ yourselves to every _____ of man for the Lord's _____, whether to the king as supreme, or to _____, as to those who are sent by _____ for the punishment of _____ and *for the* _____ of those who do _____" (1 Peter 2:13-14).

God's minister v. 4 - literally "God's servant." *From the Theological Dictionary of the New Testament, we read. "At the root of its meaning, we discover the action of the servant is to the benefit of the multitude which he serves."* In this particular setting, even *"heathen authorities can also be called the servants of God in the discharge of their office, since they are appointed by God and have the task of maintaining God's order in the world (Romans 13:1–4).* In the secular sense, regardless of the servant's faith or lack thereof, they are appointed by God, serve at His pleasure, and according to His will, they restrain evil - they keep it in check. In that sense, the protection of life and property and the preservation of order are in view.

Review Romans 13:4 and answer the following.

"He" is what, to you for good?

If you do evil, what should you be? Why? Be specific.

avenger to execute wrath v. 4 - person divinely appointed to exact punishment on those who practice evil. Note: the following definitions come from the *Greek-English Lexicon of the New Testament*.

"***avenger*** - 'justice giver;' executor of divine judgment duly appointed by God."

"***execute*** - put a plan, order, etc. into effect - perform. In the legal sense, to carry out a judicial sentence, the terms of a will, or other order."

"***wrath*** - In the Bible, we find many accounts of pagan peoples and rulers that God used to execute His wrath. From the *Theological Dictionary of the New Testament*, "*wrath is especially [sic] oriented to revenge or punishment. Wrath in this context is essentially and intentionally orientated to its content, namely, revenge or punishment. It is always seen to be protecting something recognized to be right. From a political perspective, wrath becomes a characteristic and legitimate attitude of the ruler who avenges injustice. The relation of political power to the wrath of God is to be seen in the same light. In Romans 13:4, it is obvious that political power is presented as the 'executor of divine wrath.'* " Therefore, the phrase "avenger to execute wrath" might well be translated: "justice giver to perform God's punishment for evil and or injustice."

Romans 13:1-7 highlight **the believer's obligation and responsibility to obedience to those God has called into positions of authority**, whoever they might be. (Emphasis added.) Our allegiance to God does not nullify our duty or obligation to obey the law. Instead, since God raises up those who govern us as His authority, we express obedience to God when we obey them. **The only time disobedience would be permitted would be if their requirements caused you to**

willfully sin against God by carrying out deeds or actions that would be sinful regardless of their origin. As we have already seen, Peter had some interesting words to say on the matter. (See 1 Peter 2:13-17).

fulfilled the law v. 8*; fulfillment of the law* v. 10 - literally complete, satisfy. From the *Greek-English Lexicon of the New Testament* "to provide for by supplying a complete amount—'to provide for completely, to supply fully.'" In Romans 13:8;10, love is in view. We are to love others in a way that honors God. When we do so, His commandments are satisfied. It's accomplished in loving "our neighbor" as ourselves. When we love our neighbors as ourselves harming them would never come to mind. When we love them as ourselves, this not only pleasing God and honors Him, it "*fulfills, completes, and satisfies*" God's commandments. Paul intends to show us that "authority" is not the only purveyor of peace. The love of God brings peace and keeps us in check. Read Matthew 7:12 and James 2:8. Record James 2:8 below.

James 2:8

armor of light v. 12 - We are in a battle; believers are at war against evil and darkness. Therefore, we are to dress accordingly. We are to wear suitable armor to protect ourselves, first and then for the benefit of the gospel to the dying world around us.

In ancient Rome, the armor was made of metal that reflected the sun's brilliance. The word armor, **hoplon** in Greek, means in its simplest, purest form *weapons or tools*. In this case, our weapons or armor of light reflect our new identity in Christ.

Therefore, adorn yourself with weapons that display the light of Christ in your life. If we are children of God, should we not dress like it, live like it, and be appropriately fitted to fight like it? For ourselves first, but for the benefit of the gospel as well? Paraphrasing the words of pastor and theologian John Piper, we have an obligation since we are already God's chosen ones, God's holy ones, God's loved ones, to reflect the nature and character of Christ. Paul says, put on the character that reflects your new identity. Paul admonished the Church at Colossi, "Put on then, as God's chosen ones, holy and beloved, <u>compassion, kindness, humility, meekness, and patience</u>" (Colossians 3:12) ESV. (Emphasis added.) Piper continued, "Look like Christ. Get up from your slumber or lethargy, and in juxtaposition to the "works of darkness," put on Christ. After all, He [the Lord Jesus Christ] is our *"armor of light."*

The questions before us should be this. "Are we properly dressed for protection, for battle, and love?" What should the well-dressed believer adorn this season and every season?" There is only one answer. He must put on Christ, of course!

Summarizing Romans 13:8-14, one theologian admonished believers saying, "The time has come to wake up and get dressed and love your neighbor as you love yourself." The armor of light displays the character of Christ, and it can be summed up in one word - love. For God's definition of love, let's review Paul's words to the Church at Corinth from 1 Corinthians 13:4-8.

"Love _____ long and is _____; love does not _____; love does not _____ _____, is not _____ _____; does not behave _____, does not _____ _____ _____, is not _____, thinks no _____; does not rejoice in _____, but rejoices in the _____; bears all things, _____ all things, _____ all things, _____ all things. Love _____ _____" (1 Corinthians 13:4-8).

Look at this impressive list of traits that identify love. **Love suffers long; is kind; does not envy; does not parade (or exalt) itself; is not puffed up (prideful); is not rude; not self-seeking; is not provoked (to anger); thinks no evil; does not rejoice or celebrate iniquity (sin); rejoices in truth; bears all things; believes all things; hopes all things; and endures all things - it will never fail.** Does this describe the way you love? As you consider that question, it's important to consider our dependence on God for success in all areas of faithfulness, particularly in the area of love.

Apart from the Holy Spirit, we can't "love" this way. That's in a way that honors God. But, when you yield your life daily to God, His love, which flows directly from the cross, fills you up to overflowing and, then, spills out. What happens when it spills out? It touches the lives of others!

Clothed in Christ and empowered by His Spirit, you are prepared to love your neighbor as yourself.

Even though we are sometimes unloving, we can do this. We can love like Jesus when we yield to His Spirit. Therefore, review the list again. Underline the area(s) of love that is difficult for you presently. Commit to pray over this area(s) of concern until God changes your heart. He is in the business of replacing our hearts of stone with pliable hearts of clay. Rejoice, you're in good hands; only God can shape a Christian heart by filling it with His love.

♥ Heart-Check For Today

Are you dressed in the armor of light? Pray to be clothed in His righteousness, adequately prepared for protection and battle. That's what the well-dress soldiers in God's army are wearing. It is always fashionable, never goes out of style, and fits perfectly. Putting on Christ, God's armor prepares us for whatever comes our way, including loving our neighbor as ourselves, which fulfills the law. We should "put on the Lord Jesus Christ!"

put on the Lord Jesus Christ v. 14 – *"put on"* in this verse references our sanctification, which begins the moment salvation comes, by grace through faith, and continues throughout our lives. The sanctification process transforms us little by little into the likeness of Christ. As we "put on" Christ, we "take-off" our old sinful nature. The image Paul had in view includes our thoughts and behavior. *From the Greek-English Lexicon of the New Testament, we find at its root meaning – " 'to clothe, to dress, to put on' - to put on clothes, without implying any particular article of clothing."*

Subsequently, what we chose to put on either adorns us and makes us more beautiful or deforms us, bringing dishonor upon us. Calvin, a reformer of old, said it like this. "Now to *put on* Christ, means here to be on every side fortified by the power of his Spirit, and be thereby prepared to discharge all the duties of holiness; for thus is the image of God renewed in us, which is the only true ornament of the soul."[4] Simply stated, this metaphor is a reminder to all believers that our outward beauty - that which is seen by others - should reflect the inward beauty of the transformed life of Christ.

As you conclude today's lesson, prayerfully review Paul's encouraging words to the Galatians.

---

4 Calvin, J., & Owen, J. (2010). *Commentary on the Epistle of Paul the Apostle to the Romans* (p. 490). Bellingham, WA: Logos Bible Software.

"For you are all sons of God through faith in Christ Jesus. For as many of you as were baptized into Christ have put on Christ. There is neither Jew nor Greek, there is neither slave nor free, there is neither male nor female; for you are all one in Christ Jesus. And if you *are* Christ's, then you are Abraham's seed, and heirs according to the promise" Galatians 3:26-29).

Lesson 18: Submission To Authorities & Loving Like Christ
Romans 13:1-14

Day Three: **Receive**. Review Romans 13:1-14

Memory Verse: "...and if there is any other commandment, are all summed up in this saying, namely, "You shall love your neighbor as yourself." Love does no harm to a neighbor; therefore love is the fulfillment of the law" (Romans 13:9(a)-10).

Prayerfully review Romans 13:8-14 and answer the following.

1. Review Romans 13:8. What are we to owe? Be specific.

2. In Pauline fashion, Paul turns to the Old Testament to quote scripture. In Roman 13:9, Paul reaches back to Exodus 20 and Deuteronomy 5 to highlight some specific commandments from God. They are summed up in *"loving your neighbor as yourself."* Please list each commandment recorded before the summary commandment.

    a.

    b.

    c.

    d.

e.

3. From your thoughts, define the words from the commandments quoted in Romans 13:9. Again, please Do Not Use A Dictionary. To the best of your knowledge, what do these words mean?

adultery -

murder -

steal -

bear false witness -

covet -

4 Review Romans 13:9-10. How is the fulfillment of the law accomplished? Be specific. As part of your answer, please record verse 10 below.

5. Read Luke's parable of the good Samaritan from Luke 10:25-37. Who is your neighbor?

♥ Heart-Check For Today

6. Noted theologian, pastor, and author John Piper had this to say in his book, *What Jesus Demands From The World,* concerning identifying *our neighbor*. "When we are done establishing, 'Is this my neighbor?' the decisive issue of love remains. There is a deeper question to ponder. 'What kind of person am I?'"

Before you move forward, prayerfully ponder that question. Since you have clearly defined your neighbor in question 5, who are you? In other words, what kind of person are you? Do you like who you are in the area of love? Are you yielding to the Spirit by allowing Him to bring God's Word to performance in your life? Are you being transformed into the **loving** image of Jesus, to the usefulness of God, and for the benefit of the gospel? You can sum it up with one question. "Are you about the Father's business?" That means, "Do you love after a pattern modeled by Christ?" Be honest, God already knows.

7. When we lack love, who suffers most? Do you have a testimony to share when you were found lacking love? What was the outcome? You are invited to share.

8. Thinking biblically, when we fail to *"love our neighbor as ourselves,"* what is at stake or in jeopardy?

9. In Romans 13:11, the believer is cautioned concerning *"knowing the time"* and because it's *"high time"* to do something. But, what and why? Examine the verse and complete each phrase below. From verse 11, we (believers) are:

to:_____

for now:_____

10. Again, review Romans 13:11. After careful examination of the verse, what does "knowing the time" mean? What does this verse speak to you personally?

11. Because the night is far spent and the day is at hand, what does Paul instruct? Record his specific instruction in the remainder of Romans 13:12.

12. Read and review Romans 13:13. Thinking biblically, what does it mean to walk properly, as in the day?

13. Read and review Romans 13:14. When we put on the Lord Jesus Christ, what happens and what is avoided?

Lesson 18: Submission To Authorities & Loving Like Christ
Romans 13:1-14

Day Four: **Reflect**. Prayerfully Review Romans 13:1-14

Memory Verse: "...and if there is any other commandment, are all summed up in this saying, namely, "You shall love your neighbor as yourself." Love does no harm to a neighbor; therefore love is the fulfillment of the law" (Romans 13:9(a)-10).

1. As we reflect on the fourteen verses of Romans 13, naturally, law and order come to mind. Generally speaking, God has appointed or placed authorities over us. That means believers and pagans alike are called and serve at the Lord's pleasure to maintain order and prevent chaos and anarchy. God has appointed them not to harm us or burden us with restrictions and boundaries but instead for our protection and good or well-being. Therefore, it is our responsibility to obey them as an extension of obedience to Him.

Think about those who exercise authority over your life. In the space below, make a brief list of all those who exercise Godly authority over your life.

2. Has God called you to serve as an authority over others? If so, make a brief list below of all those whom God has placed under your charge and protection.

3. If God has appointed you as an authority, remember, it's a privilege shrouded in responsibility. Are you exercising your power in a way that honors and glorifies Him? Yes or no? Circle your reply. Note: If you're not, pray and align your thinking with God. He is a merciful master.

4. We learn and grow from our mistakes. If and when we fail, God always gives us another chance to get it right. He sanctifies us over time, and because He is merciful and gracious, we get a "do-over." What's its purpose? God is merciful, and He will bring the same circumstances into our lives until we learn His ways. We must remember, too, that sanctification is a lengthy process - it takes a lifetime - and God is never in a hurry. Can you recall a time when you did not exercise your God-given authority in a way that honored Him? Did God give you a "do-over"? If so, please record your brief testimony below.

♥ Heart-Check For Today

5. Overall, how are you doing in the area of authority? Are you obedient to it? And, when you serve in an authoritative capacity, are you exercising that authority in a way that honors Jesus? Ex. Are you extending God's grace to others since He has been most gracious to you?

6. In Romans 13:8-10, Paul moves into instruction on loving your neighbor. Read the passages and record the commandment or instruction from each verse below.

v. 8

v. 9

v. 10

7. In your own words, what does it mean to love your neighbor? Do you recall a time when you demonstrated God's love for a neighbor in an unexpected way? If so, what was the outcome? Ex. How has it changed your relationship?

8. Loving your neighbor as yourself goes beyond gentle politeness and common courtesy. Jesus wants us to go above and beyond what would be the norm. He is talking about going the extra mile and truly loving your neighbor as yourself.

Here's what He said about loving others. Jesus spoke these words just before He shared the parable of the Good Samaritan in Luke 10. (See Luke 10:25-37.) According to Jesus, loving others as ourselves is linked to eternal life. In Luke 10:25, a lawyer inquired of Jesus, "Teacher, what shall I do to inherit eternal life?" Jesus' response comes from Luke 10:26-28.

"He said to him, 'What is written in the _____? What is your reading *of it?*'" So he answered and said, '*You shall* _____ *the Lord* your God with all your _____, with all your_____ with all your _____, and with all your _____,' and

_____ ' _____ _____
_____.' " And He said to him, "You have answered rightly; do this and you will _____" (Luke 10:26-28).

9. Although it may seem burdensome, we are commanded to love our neighbor as ourselves. If you're not doing it already, how do you plan to love your neighbor as yourself? Before you respond, prayerfully review Jesus' Words from Luke 10:25-37 (if you haven't already) as well as His message in Matthew 22:37-40.

10. As you close today's lesson, you're invited to give an example that reflects each aspect of love below. Ex. Does loving with all your heart involve sacrifice, humility, or dying to self? Maybe to you, it means something altogether different. If so, is there a passage of scripture that supports your answer? After prayerful consideration, and in your own words, please share what it means to love the Lord with:

All your heart?

All your soul?

All your mind?

All your strength?

As yourself?

Lesson 18: Submission To Authorities & Loving Like Christ
Romans 13:1-14

Day Five: **Respond**. Review Romans 13:1-14

Memory Verse: "…and if there is any other commandment, are all summed up in this saying, namely, "You shall love your neighbor as yourself." Love does no harm to a neighbor; therefore love is the fulfillment of the law" (Romans 13:9(a)-10).

1. Read and review Romans 13:11. What does Paul mean when he says, "for now our salvation is nearer than when we first believed?" Does this invoke a sense of urgency?

2. Thinking biblically, what are the "works of darkness" that Paul referenced in Romans 13:12?

3. What is the "armor of light?" A review of **Day Two: Research** will aid your response.

4. In essence, Paul has warned us that time is short. In light of that statement, read and review Romans 13:14. As believers, we respond in faith by "putting on Christ, thereby making no provision for the flesh and fulfilling its lusts."

   a. How have you "put on" Christ?

   b. Thinking biblically, what is meant by Paul's instructions to "make no provision for the flesh, to fulfill its lusts"?

5. Thinking biblically, why might making no provision for the fulfilling fleshly lusts be necessary?

6. Believers are often subject to harsh judgment, scrutiny, and criticism. The world is watching us with a critical eye at all times. Since we are in the spotlight, if we fail to "put on" the Lord Jesus Christ, what is at stake?

7. Have you failed in the area of "putting on the Lord Jesus Christ?" If so, you are invited to share a brief testimony concerning this failure. Be sure to include God's merciful response and restoration in your testimony.

Each day as we "put on" the Lord Jesus Christ, we are prepared for whatever comes our way. Remember, we are soldiers in the army of God. Do you pause to "put on" Christ each day? If not, pledge to make this a routine as you physically dress each morning. Get a visual in your mind of adorning yourself with Christ. Over time, you will see that this is not only biblical; it's a precious privilege to do so. Only the redeemed of God can clothe themselves in Christ and His righteousness. As you fill your heart and mind with Christ, then you are appropriately clothed and prepared to partner with Jesus to be about the Father's business.

8. As we conclude our study in Romans 13, we respond by "putting on" the Lord Jesus Christ. As His children, we have all that we need. There is victory in Jesus! You are invited to close in a prayer of adoration, confession, thanksgiving, and supplication. Are you not blessed to know that as His child, you can get up each day and "put on" the Lord Jesus Christ? What could be more impressive than that? You may record your four-part prayer below.

On this date _____, this was my heart felt prayer:

of adoration:

of confession:

of thanksgiving:

Prayer of supplication:

Words from Jesus
"Blessed are those who hunger and thirst for righteousness,
For they shall be filled" (Matthew 5:6).

Lesson 19: Finding Unity In The Love Of Christ
Romans 14:1-23

Day One: **Read.** Prayerfully Read Romans 14:1-23

Memory Verse: "Therefore do not let your good be spoken of as evil; for the kingdom of God is not eating and drinking, but righteousness and peace and joy in the Holy Spirit" (Romans 14:16-17).

Believers come from diverse backgrounds, and some enjoy and celebrate Christian liberty more freely than others. That statement has been true since the first-century believers broke bread together, and it's still true, even today. That's because we are unique individuals with diverse backgrounds and beliefs about food and drink. Like the Jews, many of us are passionate about traditions and our beliefs. Some of us cling to strict boundaries and feel horrible, even to self-condemnation, if and when we break our self-imposed restrictions. We must remember, things like this have absolutely nothing to do with salvation.

It's not about what we eat and drink or how we dress or if we do or don't cut our hair, or whether we dance or don't. Rifts causing division, strife, and church splits have occurred over nonsensical and irrelevant concerns. Christ has done it all. We are not keeping the law. Remember, we are saved by faith – period! Nonetheless, these issues, as well as other do's and don'ts, will plague the family of faith until Christ's glorious return.

The Romans struggled, as many of us do. Their hot debates reached a fever pitch. The arguments over dietary issues threatened the unity within the body. As a result, judgment, discord, and criticism crept in. What was the problem? Among its members, Jewish Christians were reluctant to give up certain ceremonial aspects of their religious heritage. Moreover, they were uncertain about how faith in Christ affected the status of the Old Testament regulations.

In other words, the Old Testament law pushed against grace, which was celebrated by many of the new covenant believers. According to Peter's vision, everything was clean. No food was off the menu. However, It was such a divisive issue that Paul was prompted to instruct the entire body of believers concerning their scriptural responsibility. In Romans 13, Paul spoke passionately about our responsibility and command to love one another and fulfill the law. Most assuredly, that would include overlooking dietary issues and putting an end to long debates over what believers eat and drink. Selfish pride was to be replaced by humility, love, and faith in God. After all, God had received them all, and our personal opinions, which generally favor our predispositions, are irrelevant to God.

According to Paul, all things in moderation are acceptable. As we shall see, if our hearts do not condemn us, it's not sinning. However, several things must be considered when we look at abstention. Four immediately come to mind. They are: 1.) Motivation, 2.) Self-righteousness, 3.) Pride, and 4.) Judgment. If Paul were here, he might ask, "Who are we to judge the Spirit's work in another?" We are all saved by grace through faith, and God is prepared to strip us of everything to accomplish His goal. What's His goal? Ultimately, it's conforming us to the image of His Son. Therefore, let God be God! To paraphrase Jesus, **It's not what we put into the body that defiles a man. Instead, it's what comes out of His heart that condemns him.** (See Matthew 15:10-20).

One final thought on food and wine. If abstention of certain things is to earn favor with God, how much more grace or favor do you think He can extend? Remember, His electing love has already chosen and called you out of death and darkness and into His marvelous light. You are His and a co-heir with Jesus to all that God can give. Your sins are forgiven, you have Christ's righteousness, and your eternal destiny is secure. One day, you will be with Jesus in heaven. But more than that, you will be like Him too!

To sum it up, **the Christian life has never been based on what we/you can do or give. Instead, it's entirely based on what Christ has done on our/your behalf.** Make it personal. We must be careful lest we fall into the mindset that we can give something to God or give something up for God. He is looking for our faith in Him alone. Abraham "believed God," and it was credited to him as righteousness. Believing God was enough for Abraham, and although He was not perfect, he was God's man. He, too, was called and chosen just like you! God delighted in their fellowship, so much so that He has called Abraham "friend." That was enough for Abraham. Is it sufficient for you?

1. Read Romans 14:1. Believers are instructed to do two things. List them below.

    a.

    b.

2. From Romans 14:2, who eats only vegetables?

3. Read and review Romans 14:3. What is revealed about the heart?

4. Read and review Romans 14:4. Then, explain the question, the answer, and the verse's meaning in the space below.

    a. the question:

    b. the answer:

    c. the meaning:

5. From Romans 14:5, what is the controversy?

6. Read Romans 14:6.

   a. What is being observed or not?

   b. Thinking biblically, what does that mean?

7. From Romans 14:6, complete the following.

"He who eats, eats to the Lord, for he gives God _____; and he who does not eat, to the Lord he does not eat, and gives God _____" (Romans 14:6).

8. What is the common denominator in verse 6? _____

9. The Christian life has never been about oneself or an inward focus. We have died to self, remember? If we say, "I only have one life to live, and I'll live it as I see fit," we are way off track. We have been bought or redeemed at a premium price. We belong to God! A better statement would be, "I regret that I only have one life to give!" As believers, we should endeavor to glorify God and please Him in all things. (See 1 Corinthians 10:13.) Prayerfully read Romans 14:7 and 1 Corinthians 6:20. Complete each verse below.

"For none of us _____ to himself, and no one _____ to himself" (Romans 14:7).

"For _____ were _____ at a price; therefore _____ God in your _____ and in your _____, which are God's" (1 Corinthians 6:20).

10. From Romans 14:8, in whom do we live and die? _____

11. Read and review Romans 14:9-11 and answer the following questions.

   a. According to Paul, what two things do we do to our brother?

b. In the coming days, where shall we all stand?

c. From Romans 14:11, "As I live," the Lord says what? Record the remainder of verse 11 for your answer. (Note: These are quotes from Isaiah 45:23; 49:18.)

12. Paul concludes this section with an essential reminder to believers in Romans 14:12-13.

   a. What is it?

   b. As a result, what is Paul's valuable conclusion? Be specific.

13. Paraphrase the advice given in Romans 14:14.

   Phrase One:

   Phrase Two:

♥ Heart-Check For Today

14. What was Paul attempting to accomplish within the church through his warning and instructions? Why would this be important? Make it personal. Is it important to you today? Prayerfully consider your response. You are invited to share.

As we bring today's lesson to its end, issues concerning food and drink should be settled in your heart and mind. If not, seek God's guidance on the matter as you prayerfully reread Romans 14. Then, if concerns remain, ask for guidance from your Bible study leader or pastor. Remember, too, that "eating and drinking" has been a hotbed of contention since Paul penned Romans, even though neither one can, or will, affect your salvation.

In some denominations, "eating and drinking" remains an area of concern. Although we are no longer keeping the law, some are over-burdened with "don'ts" regardless. Remember, too, that you are not your neighbor. You will give an accounting for you – not your neighbor and vice versa.

When you are satisfied that your decisions are coming from faith – go with it. With peace and confidence, let your conscience guide you. Then, trust God and allow Him to sort it all out. You can't bring others along, but God can. He is able and willing to handle all of His children and administer the necessary liberty, discipline, or correction as need be. His arm is not short, and He is not shy or slow concerning His divine purposes. The loving eye of God sees all things. Too, He hears all things and knows all things. Thankfully, His plan will not be thwarted.

Lesson 19: Finding Unity In The Love Of Christ
Romans 14:1-23

Day Two: **Research**. Review Romans 14:1-23

Memory Verse: "Therefore do not let your good be spoken of as evil; for the kingdom of God is not eating and drinking, but righteousness and peace and joy in the Holy Spirit" (Romans 14:16-17).

I. Using a bible, bible dictionary, or concordance define the following *key words.*

judge vv. 3, 4, 10, 12, 13, *judgment* v. 10 -

contempt v. 10 -

grieved v. 15 -

peace v. 17 -

joy v. 17 -

edify v. 19 -

condemn v. 22; *condemned* v. 23 -

II. Read the following *key phrases.*

stumbling block v. 13 - *From the Greek-English Lexicon of the New Testament, "an occasion or reason for taking offense—'something to cause offense, what causes someone to be offended, offense.'"* The common thought among most conservative theologians is this. A stumbling block is anything a believer does—even though the Bible may permit it—that causes another to fall into sin. For clarity, read 1 Corinthians 8:9 and Romans 14:20.

walking in love v. 15 –

walking - Generally speaking, *"walking"* in this verse references how we live. From the *Greek-English Lexicon of the New Testament, "'walking' is to live or behave in a customary manner, with possible focus upon continuity of action—'to live, to behave, to go about doing.'"*

in love - Believers are to "go" about in love. The movement of the believer is in view. **Love** in this verse is agape. From the *Greek-English Lexicon of the New Testament,* agape love means *"to have love for someone or something, based on sincere appreciation and high regard—'to love, to regard with affection, loving concern, love.'"* In Romans 13, Paul has given instruction which reminds us that love is the fulfillment of the law. The heart of the law is found in Romans 13:8-10. From this passage, failure to regard a weaker brother or sister's dietary restrictions violated the *"law of love."* Such judgment, criticism, or general lack of disregard was unloving and unacceptable among those in whom Christ's love abounds.

Paul reaches back to four of the Ten Commandments to further demonstrate that love fulfills the law. Paul instructed. "Owe no one anything except to love one another, for he who loves another has fulfilled the law." For the commandments, *"You shall not commit adultery," "You shall not murder," "You shall not steal," "You shall not bear false witness," "You shall not covet,..."* (Romans 13:8-9(a).

Complete Romans 13:9(b)-10 below.

"...and if there is any other commandment, are *all* summed up in this saying, namely, 'You shall love your neighbor as yourself.'_____

_____."

kingdom of God v. 16 - According to *Easton's Bible Dictionary*, the *"kingdom of Christ and of God," the "kingdom of David," "the kingdom," and the "kingdom of heaven, all reference or express the same thing under different aspects. These include, but are not limited to:*

- *Christ's authority as mediator, or His rule on the earth;*
- *The blessings and advantages of all kinds that flow from His rule;*
- *The subjects of this kingdom, taken collectively, or the Church.*

According to Matthew Henry, *"the nature of true Christianity, is here called, The kingdom of God; it is a religion intended to rule us, a kingdom: it stands in true and hearty subjection to God's power and dominion. The gospel dispensation is in a special manner called the kingdom of God..."*[5]

A conservative Bible expositor noted this is referencing the kingdom of God, *"The kingdom of God is the sphere of salvation where God rules in the hearts of those He has saved."* Others have referenced it as *"righteous living,"* and *"that which reigns within you, not an outward performance or display, rather utter joy in the heart which frees us from sin and guilt. Utter joy is the hallmark trait of the citizens of God's kingdom."*

For clarity, let's examine three passages from the New Testament which reference the Kingdom of God. Prayerfully review Matthew 6:33; Mark 1:14-15; and Luke 4:43 to discover what Jesus has said about His Kingdom, which is the Kingdom of God.

From John 18:36
Jesus answered, "My kingdom is not of this world. If My kingdom were of this world, My servants would fight, so that I should not be delivered to the Jews; but now My kingdom is not from here." (Emphasis added.)

From Mark 1:14-15
Now after John was put in prison, Jesus came to Galilee, preaching the gospel of the kingdom of God, and saying, "The time is fulfilled, and the kingdom of God is at hand. Repent, and believe in the gospel." (Emphasis added.)

---

5   Henry, Matthew (1706). *Matthew Henry's Commentary on the Whole Bible: Volume VI-I Acts – Romans* (p.450). Devoted Publishing, Woodstock, Ontario, Canada 2018

From Luke 4:43

"I must preach the kingdom of God to the other cities also, because for this purpose I have been sent." (Emphasis added.)

Not to oversimplify, but the kingdom of God is comprised of those called and chosen by God who has heard the gospel message, received it into their hearts, having come to saving faith, and now live under the love, power, and authority of God. They are "governed by God." They not only accept His authority but live in peace and joy, filled with His Spirit. These are the chosen – God's elect – the recipients of His divine favor, grace, and blessings.

Lesson 19: Finding Unity In The Love Of Christ
Romans 14:1-23

Day Three: **Receive.** Review Romans 14:1-23

Memory Verse: "Therefore do not let your good be spoken of as evil; for the kingdom of God is not eating and drinking, but righteousness and peace and joy in the Holy Spirit" (Romans 14:16-17).

1. From Romans 14:14, what does The Lord Jesus convince Paul and why?

2. Read Romans 14:15. If your food grieves your brother, what happens?

3. What warning is found in the second phrase of Romans 14:15? Record the phrase below.

4. Review Romans 14:16. If you do not heed Paul's warning, what is the consequence? Thinking biblically, what is at stake?

5. In Romans 14:17, Paul says the kingdom of God is not two things. What are they?

   a.

   b.

6. Reread Romans 14:17, the kingdom of God is three things. What are they? Be specific.

   a.

   b.

   c.

7. From Romans 14:18, who is acceptable to God and approved by men? For your answer, record the verse below.

Romans 14:18

8. Read and review Romans 14:19. What is suggested? Write the verse in your own words without losing its meaning.

9. What is the central message of Romans 14:19?

10. Paul gives warning and encouragement in Romans 14:20. What was Paul's message?

11. Paul suggests that something is evil in Romans 14:20. What is it? Be specific.

12. Read and review Romans 14:21. What may cause your brother to stumble?

13. Read and review Romans 14:22-23 and answer the following.

   a. Who is happy? Be specific.

   b. Who is condemned? Be specific.

14. Record the words of Romans 14:23 below.

Romans 14:23 –

Lesson 19: Finding Unity In The Love Of Christ
Romans 14:1-23

Day Four: **Reflect**. Prayerfully Review Romans 14:1-23

Memory Verse: "Therefore do not let your good be spoken of as evil; for the kingdom of God is not eating and drinking, but righteousness and peace and joy in the Holy Spirit" (Romans 14:16-17).

Like churches today, the family of faith in Rome was made up of both weak and strong believers. Their weakness or strength had nothing to do with their longevity in salvation. Instead, it referenced their conscience and letting go of ceremonial rites. Among other things, the weak believers struggled to abandon dietary laws and their strict observance of the Sabbath. They were also conflicted by their continuing desire to offer sacrifices in the temple.

That was in stark contrast to stronger believers who seemed not to struggle with rites and rituals of the past. They transitioned from the law into grace with much celebration and freedom. They abandoned all the former religious ceremonies and rituals and embraced their newfound liberty. They ate and drank whatever they desired because everything was considered clean. They had loosed all restrictions regarding the Sabbath and embraced Jesus' words, "that the Sabbath was made for man, not man for the Sabbath." (See Mark 2:27.) For the weaker believers, the most significant offense of the stronger may have been their consumption of cheaper meat from the marketplace, regardless of whether or not it had been offered to idols. In contrast, their weaker brothers and sisters ate a "vegetarian diet" to ensure no contact with anything remotely related to sin. Their past life of keeping 613 rules and regulations had a lingering hold over their lives.

On both sides, their sensibilities ran amuck. Each believed they were right, and their brothers and sisters were wrong. But, it was more than that. Mostly, they found the practices of their non-conforming brothers and sisters in Christ offensive. If you were weak, you were appalled by the stronger. And if you were strong, you dismissed the weaker or more vulnerable for their lack of liberty and understanding of grace. Needless to say, it was a hotbed for contention, which fueled division, judgment, and criticism. What's the bottom line? They all lacked love; they withheld mercy even though God had been merciful to all of them. They were desensitized to the other's feelings, and they were all guilty of "not loving their neighbor as themselves." Nor were they concerned about the possibility of causing their brothers or sisters to stumble. In short, they had failed in the second-highest commandment - to love your neighbor as yourself. Paul addresses these issues in Romans 14.

Paul's assessment of the Jewish converts at the church in Rome is descriptive rather than judgmental. Read and review Romans 14:1-4 and answer the following questions.

1. Read Romans 14:1. What were they not to dispute over?

2. From Romans 14:2, what is the issue with food?

3. Read Romans 14:3. What is Paul's advice? Record the verse below.

Romans 14:3 –

4. Paul asks a question in Romans 14:4. In your opinion, what is the root of Paul's question?

5. Thinking biblically, when, if ever, would it be right to judge another believer or their servant? If possible, record a verse in support of your answer.

6. We bring previous orientations, traditions, and habits with us when we come to faith in Christ. The general idea is that we come as we are - baggage and all. Our transformation comes about gradually. Over time, the sanctification process enables us to open our hands and release all nonessential details that don't enhance our lives in Christ. The Holy Spirit deals with us gently and patiently, which reflects Christ's very nature. He is never cross, judgmental, or threatening in the process. He renews our minds through the revelation of scripture. Consequently, the things that once proved vitally important become of little value in light of our increasing knowledge and revelation of Jesus.

As stronger sisters in the faith, we should welcome weaker ones in love rather than despise them or treat them with contempt because of their previous orientations. We must allow God's Word, which is empowered by His Spirit, to do its perfect work. That means to let God be God. God has received them (as He did you), and He, alone, can make His servants stand. We must prayerfully encourage their journey and speak the truth in love. God's truth is never judgmental or critical – it's truthful – period. We are to model Christ and love them through the process. Has He not loved you through the same process? Yes or no? Please circle your answer.

7. Perhaps you had previous orientations, traditions, or habits that were difficult to overcome when you came to faith. If so, how did the liberty of others affect you? In the space below, please provide several descriptive words which define that time in your journey.

8. Thinking back, how did stronger believers in the faith receive you? If you can recall, please provide several descriptive words which describe how you were received when you were new in the faith.

9. God has received them into the family of faith - just as they are. Lest you forget, He has similarly accepted you. Therefore, as His purveyors of love and grace upon the earth, we must accept them just as they are, too. Remember, our acceptance and love for them are required, and doing so fulfills the law. We are commanded to love rather than judge. First, read and record James 4:12 below. Next, prayerfully read Mark 12:30-31 to hear God's heart.

James 4:12 –

"And you shall love the Lord your God with all your heart, with all your soul, with all your mind, and with all your strength. This *is* the first commandment. And the second, like *it, is* this: *'You shall love your neighbor as yourself.'* There is no other commandment greater than these" (Mark 12:30-31).

10. The family of faith has much diversity. Each member was called and chosen by God before the foundation of the world. His choice was purposeful and intentional and had eternity in view. The family of faith is a beautiful melting pot whose fragrance reaches to the heavens proclaiming the goodness of our Great God and Savior Jesus Christ, our Lord. The church is to His praise and glory! We are called to unity in Christ, and nonessential details which divide us must be left at the

door. Why would unity be so essential within the body? Thinking biblically, if we are not united, what's at stake?

11. How can we effectively reach, love, and serve those outside the church if we can't do it effectively, and with the purity of heart, among our brothers and sisters in Christ who are among us? Are you loving like Christ and overlooking unnecessary details?

12. Read and review Romans 14:9-11. Two crucial questions are asked in these passages. Do you see them? Record them below.

   Question #1

   Question #2

13. There is no room in the church to pass judgment on one another. We have a righteous judge. Who is it? _____. Record the last phrase of Romans 14: 10 below.

v. 10

♥ Heart-Check For Today

14. According to Romans 14:17, the kingdom of God is not about eating and drinking! Over time, our faith in Christ will be revealed, for it is demonstrated in the way we live. One commentator said it like this, "In the long run, the validity of faith is established by the quality of life it produces. What people do is the most accurate indicator of what they truly believe." In your opinion, does your life evidence what you believe? If not, what do you plan to do about it?

15. After quoting Isaiah 45:23 in Romans 14:11, Paul summarizes this portion of his message in Romans 14:12-13. Complete Paul's summary statement below.

"So then each of us shall give _____ of himself to God. Therefore let us not _____ one another anymore, but rather resolve this, not to put a _____ _____ or a cause to _____ in our brother's way" (Romans 14:12-13).

Lesson 19: Finding Unity In The Love Of Christ
Romans 14:1-23

Day Five: **Respond**. Review Romans 14:1-23

Memory Verse: "Therefore do not let your good be spoken of as evil; for the kingdom of God is not eating and drinking, but righteousness and peace and joy in the Holy Spirit" (Romans 14:16-17).

The church in Rome was found lacking. They had come up short in the area of love, even though love is the guide for all Christian conduct. As a result, the unity was destroyed, and the church as a whole had fallen far short of demonstrating faithfulness and fulfilling the law through love.

Before we respond to God's word, today's lesson will unpack the law of love to discover God's plan for authentic love within the family of faith. Although some of the passages in chapter 14 may appear redundant, they serve an essential function. Paul knew that repetition and reinforcement (from God's Spirit) would be required to change hearts and the prevailing attitudes within the body. Just in case they missed it, Paul would drive his points home for the sake of unity and love within God's church. Their rights and personal preferences were to be laid aside in the interest of love, for the greater good, and the benefit of the gospel.

We must love one another because the non-believing world is watching us. They are looking to see that our faith is genuine. They are also looking for a reason to believe in the God of our salvation. The gospel is at stake! When we fulfill the law in love, we see the life-changing power of God's love at work. When a group of unlikely companions rub well together and esteem the needs of all others as more significant than their own - love wins! When they're found faithful by loving their neighbors well, it not only pleases God, but it testifies that God reigns and rules within us - His body - Christ's Church.

On the contrary, when a body of believers is busy infighting about nonessential details, it has lost its focus and purpose, namely love. That's what happened in Rome, but Paul's message would reach divided hearts. When love prevails, all else is trumped. Lastly, loving well changes our focus from inward to outward. Then we're united with a common goal and purpose. What's that? Always, it's advancing the gospel and partnering with God to fill His kingdom. At its core, it's the salvation of the lost. Remember, love that fulfills the law covers a multitude of sins, including yours!

1. In Romans 14:19, Paul begins to summarize his thoughts and presents a forceful solution. What two things does Paul recommend to the divided church in Rome?

Be specific.

   a.

   b.

2. Thinking biblically, why would this be necessary? What would it benefit if, instead of pleasing ourselves, we edified other believers in love? Review Romans 14:19 before you respond.

3. Read and review Romans 14:20. A church that loves well exalts the work of God, which is the salvation of the saints. We have a job to do, individually and as a body. God is a purposeful God! We were created and saved with purpose and on purpose. He has prepared a "work" for His global church from eternity past. Time is short; we must be about the Father's business!

Ephesians 2:10

♥ Heart-Check For Today

4. We are called to build up the body, not tear it down. We must never allow individual preferences or personal likes and dislikes to injure or bring to no account the work that God has done in another saint. We must never cause them to stumble or fall because, in selfish zeal, we celebrate our liberty in Christ. Remember, you're a sinner saved by grace through faith, too! You stand at the pleasure of God. You have nothing to boast or exalt but Christ! Who are you to judge? Instead, we should check our motives by these biblical principles of love. You are invited to share a brief testimony.

    a. Am I loving well?

    b. Am I esteeming all others greater than myself?

    c. Are my thoughts Christ-centered?

    d. Am I edifying others?

5. Read and complete 1 Corinthians 10:23-24 below.

"All things are _____ for _____, but not all things are _____; all things are _____ for me, but not all things _____. 24 Let no one seek his _____, but each one the _____ _____" (1 Corinthians 10:23-24).

6. In Romans 14:19, *"edify"* is the opposite of *"destroy"* in Romans 14:20. Destroy means "to destroy [tear down, ruin] completely the efforts or work of someone else—'to destroy, to ruin utterly.' "[6] Thinking biblically, how might you edify others rather than destroy them.

---

[6] Louw, J. P., & Nida, E. A. (1996). *Greek-English lexicon of the New Testament: based on semantic domains* (electronic ed. of the 2nd edition., Vol. 1, p. 233). New York: United Bible Societies.

7. When we fulfill the law in love, we bring the cross of Christ front and center. The cross always brings us back to love because, on the cross, the merciful love of God collided with the depravity of man and the power of sin, and its eternal consequences were settled forever. When the cross is in view, it changes everything. It always has. Down through the centuries, in the shadow of the cross, even the hardest hearts have been melted. Can you see the cross? Get a picture of it in your mind. In light of the cross, can you not lay your individual preferences aside? Can you not place love and Godly principles above personalities for the sake of unity, edification or building-up, and the advancement of the gospel? We are much stronger united than we are divided! The church must unite to accomplish God's work. We cannot achieve His kingdom-purposes through any other means.

Before you respond to God's word, sit for a moment, and recall the faithful members of God's church who've encouraged your journey when you were weaker in faith. Now it's your turn.

God is calling His last days' church to sacrificial love, and it's radical. Can you do it? You don't need to respond aloud; God knows your heart. If it's unloving, it needs an adjustment. Confess it, and pray! If you want to be more loving, humble yourself, seek His face, turn from sin, and God will heal you. That's the formula for all heart revivals, and it begins one heart at a time. If it's needed, allow Him to revive your heart, soul, and spirit! Go to the cross, for in the shadow of His cross, you will find the strength to love all others and fulfill the law.

You're invited to close in prayer!

Words From Jesus
"A new command I give you: Love one another.
As I have loved you, so you must love one another" (John 13:34).

Lesson 20: Paul's Closing Summation
Romans 15:1-33

Day One: **Read**. Prayerfully Read Romans 15:1-33

Memory Verse: "Now may the God of peace be with you all. Amen" (Romans 15:33).

1. Review Romans 15:1. What two things are suggested to those who are strong?

   a. We ought to:

   b. We should not:

2. From Romans 15:2, what leads to edification?

3. Read Romans 15:3. Christ did not do something. What did He not do, and what was written? Complete the last phrase of verse 3 per the instructions.

   a. Who did Christ not please?

   b. "For even Christ did not please Himself; but as it is written,_____

   _____" (Romans 15:3).

4. Read Romans 15:4 and answer the following questions:

   a. What was written for our learning?

   b. What two aspects of the scripture might produce hope?

c. In your own words, define *hope*.

5. Review Romans 15:5. Something is desired from the God of comfort and patience.

   a. What is it? According to who?

   b. Thinking biblically, why would this matter?

6. From Romans 15:6, what was this "like-mindedness" to produce among believers?

7. Paraphrase the instructive message from Romans 15:7 below.

   Therefore to the glory of God, we must:

8. Read Romans 15:8-9 and answer the following questions:

   a. Who became a servant to the circumcision?

   b. For what purpose?

   d. That the Gentiles might what?

9. Paul, an Old Testament scholar and self-proclaimed "Pharisee of Pharisees," is a master with words. In typical Pauline fashion, he encourages faithfulness by citing passages that are not so new after all. Here's an example. In Romans 15:9-12, Paul reaches back to Old Testament scriptures to remind the Jewish Christians (Messianic Jews) that salvation of the Gentiles has always been God's plan. These Old Testament words reveal God's plan from before the foundation of the world. Read the verses and complete the following questions, looking for the verbal action of each verse within each passage.

Read and Romans 15:9 and Psalm 18:49. Two action words are identified in both verses. Do you see them? Record them below. (Hint: These also appear in 2 Samuel 22:50.)

10. Read and review Romans 15:10 and Deuteronomy 32:43a. What is the verbal action of these verses?

11. Read and review Romans 15:11 and Psalm 117:1. What verbal phrase is carried forward to Romans 15?

12. Read Romans 15:12 and the Messianic promise of Isaiah 11:10. Who shall reign over the Gentiles and produce what from these verses?

   a. Who:_____

   b. To produce:_____

In Romans 15, we find three prayers or benedictions. They appear in Romans 15:4-5; 13; and 33. A benediction is "the *utterance or bestowing of a blessing over people.*" Even today, scriptural blessings are spoken over congregations during worship services, especially at their conclusion. It's a common practice among Protestant denominations. Particularly those that follow a structured liturgy (order of service) such as the Episcopal, Methodist, Lutheran, and Presbyterian denominations. With anticipation, the congregation waits for the benediction as it signals the end of the service. These verses serve as God's parting words to His people. The "blessings" promote unity and central focus. They are meant to encourage and inspire the *"body"* to unite throughout the coming week on God's parting message to His family of faith. Catholic priests also give a "priestly prayer" or benediction after each service. The word *benediction* is Old French from Latin, *"benedicere,"* meaning to *"wish well, bless."*

13. Let's conclude today's lesson with a benediction as we review the prayer of Romans 15:4-5. Herein, Paul identifies God as our source of patience and comfort (encouragement). Then, in Romans 15:13, he expands his description of God by adding *"hope"* to the blessing. Complete the words of Romans 15:13 below.

"Now may the God of _____ fill you with all _____ and _____ in believing, that you may abound in _____ by the power of the Holy Spirit" (Romans 15:13).

Lesson 20: Paul's Closing Summation
Romans 15:1-33

Day Two: **Research**. Review Romans 15:1-33

Memory Verse: "Now may the God of peace be with you all. Amen" (Romans 15:33).

I. Using a bible, bible dictionary, or concordance define the following **key words.**

reproach v. 3 –

circumcision v. 8 -

minister, ministering v. 16 -

hindered v. 22 -

debtors v. 27 -

partakers v. 27 -

strive v. 30 -

II. Read the following **key phrases.**

servant to the circumcision v. 8 - From the *Theological Dictionary of the New Testament*, we find the following definition. "When it is said in Romans 15:8 that Christ is a 'servant of the circumcision,' this merely means that Christ's work is on behalf of Israel." That references His initial work. It is expressly understood that Christ, a Jew, came first to the house of Israel. In *Paul's Greetings to the Romans* (lesson one of our Romans' study), we identified and studied the epistle's thesis verse, Romans 1:16-17. Verse 16 says, "For I am not ashamed of the gospel of Christ, for it is the power of God to salvation for everyone who believes, for the Jew first and also for the Greek."

gospel of Christ v. 29 - literally the good news of Jesus! Having read the commentary above, we are reminded of what good news the gospel of Christ truly is! The gospel is the most extraordinary story ever told. Think about it a minute; someone who was innocent and free of all sin paid your penalty and took your punishment for sin. That's the good news of the gospel. Jesus died for you while you were a sinner, an enemy of God, and a God-hater. Jesus accomplished on your behalf what you could never do for yourself. You are free and have "right standing" before God because Jesus has ransomed you. You are righteous, and He has given you His spirit. When the Father looks at you, He sees His son Jesus, the perfect lamb of sacrifice. Lastly, you have been reconciled to God, and a place in eternity is being prepared for you. One day soon, you will rule and reign with Jesus!

Note: As it relates to Romans 15, below you will find optional material explaining God's plan for salvation. If you are unfamiliar with God's covenant, the sacrifice of Jesus, or His identity as a "servant to the circumcision," a quick read is recommended.

An Explanation of God's Two-Fold Plan of Salvation

In Romans 15:8, Paul provides a two-fold explanation for Jesus coming to earth as a *"servant to the circumcision."* For further study, what did God's two-fold plan provide? Salvation, of course, for the Jews and the Gentiles.

1. **First, we see that Jesus came to prove that God is truthful and faithful to His promises.** Precisely, that's what Romans 15:8 tells us. It says that "Jesus Christ came to confirm (verify or prove to be true and certain) the promises made to the fathers..." As we begin, it's important to consider how and when the promises were made and to which father(s). So, let's take a look.

Centuries earlier, God called Abraham and awakened him spiritually. God made an irrevocable promise to His people (and all the peoples of the earth) through him. The unveiling of God's covenant begins in Genesis 12. Through each of God's revelations, the scope of the covenant or promise was expanded. Since God never gives us more than we can process, the revelations were generational. As time passed, and through each patriarch, God revealed heightened details concerning His plan.

In addition to His verbal promise, God aided it in demonstrating His pledge. He lived it out! In so doing, God revealed His desire for a relationship with His people through Abraham. In James 2:23, scripture identifies Abraham as God's friend. How very unique! Through His dealings with Abraham, including discipline, God proved His intense love for His people. That's all who come to faith – even you! Indeed, Abraham's story is unique. Not only because it preserves the record of God's steadfast love and unveils relationship with the living God, but it also exposes His providential or keeping care, His plan and sovereignty, and attention to detail in our lives.

Since that day, God has been faithful. Through Jesus' coming, His covenantal promises to Abraham are fulfilled. But it didn't end there. These irrevocable promises (and blessings) were passed from Abraham to his offspring, Next to Isaac, then to Jacob (later called Israel), and on to Joseph, etc. Christ's coming proved God's faithfulness. Indeed, He has demonstrated faithfulness, and He is worth believing! As per God's plan, many Jews believed. Remember, all the Jews who believed died in faith, looking forward to salvation through the promised One coming. That's what faith is. It's "the substance of things hoped for and the evidence of things not seen." (See Hebrews 11:1). Thankfully, faith is still faith, and that will never change, nor the means of grace by which we receive it. So, it's clear. God's promise is faithful and true!

One last thought on God's faithfulness, it didn't begin with us; instead, long ago. Some 6,000 years before, God had called Abraham and made this irrevocable promise. If you are unfamiliar with this covenantal promise, take the time to review it below. It's important because it's the Old Covenant linked to "the promises made to the fathers" of Romans 15:8.

Genesis 17 begins, "When Abram was ninety-nine years old, the LORD appeared to Abram and said to him, "I *am* Almighty God; walk before Me and be blameless. 2 And I will make My covenant between Me and you, and will multiply you exceedingly." 3 Then Abram fell on his face, and God talked with him, saying: 4 "As for Me, behold, My covenant is with you, and you shall be a father of many nations. 5 No longer shall your name be called Abram, but your name shall be Abraham; for I have made you a father of many nations. 6 I will make you exceedingly fruitful; and I will make nations of you, and kings shall come from you. 7 And I will establish My covenant between Me and you and your descendants after you in their generations, for an everlasting covenant, to be God to you and your descendants after you. 8 Also I give to you and your descendants after you the land in which you are a stranger, all the land of Canaan, as an everlasting possession; and I will be their God."

[9] And God said to Abraham: "As for you, you shall keep My covenant, you and your descendants after you throughout their generations. <u>This is My covenant which you shall keep, between Me and you and your descendants after you: Every male child among you shall be circumcised; 11 and you shall be circumcised in the flesh of your foreskins, and it shall be a sign of the covenant between Me and you. 12 He who is eight days old among you shall be circumcised, every male child in your generations, he who is born in your house or bought with money from any foreigner who is not your descendant. 13 He who is born in your house and he who is bought with your money must be circumcised, and My covenant shall be in your flesh for an everlasting covenant. 14And the uncircumcised male child, who is not circumcised in the flesh of his foreskin, that person shall be cut off from his people; he has broken My covenant</u>" (Genesis 17:1-14)(Emphasis added.)

2. **Like the first reason, the second remains. It's glorifying God.** The Bible records, "...and that the Gentiles might **glorify God for His mercy**..." (Romans 15:9)(Emphasis added.) Watch this. God has been merciful to us! What God accomplished for us through Jesus' atoning work on our behalf is the most compassionate act - ever - since time began. No other acts or actions compare, regardless of how marvelous their works appear. Only Jesus could die for our sins. In so doing, God has poured out His mercy on us, which means we get God's grace (His unearned, unmerited favor) rather than what we've earned - certain death. God has made the way of salvation. He has sent us Jesus. The name Jesus in Arabic means "God is salvation." In Hebrew, it's "Jehovah saves; God saves." For that, we (the Gentiles) glorify God for His mercy indeed.

As we read above, there was a **sign of the covenant.** What was it? It was circumcision, which was an outward symbol of an inward heart-change. Each Jew's circumcision identified them as God's chosen one. Collectively, they were a people called and chosen by God. Moreover, God required it. We know, however, that the law could never save us. It merely served as a schoolmaster to reveal our sin and our need for God. The New Covenant offered something entirely different. A circumcision would still be required, but this time the circumcision would involve the heart. Old Testament prophets spoke of this coming new day, as well. It's identified as the New Covenant.

Ezekiel's prophetic message lists several aspects of the New Covenant. Its recipients could anticipate:

1.) A new heart.
2.) A new spirit.
3.) The indwelling Holy Spirit, and
4.) True holiness for God's chosen.

Look closely at the list. Could any of *these* be provided through the Mosaic Law of the Old Testament? Of course not! Indeed, the New Covenant promised heightened intimacy and reliance on God. Additionally, it paved the way for a relationship with God which fulfilled part of His desire in creating us. What part did it fulfill? Essentially, knowing God through a loving relationship. That requires unity through an unbroken, unrivaled fellowship with God and steadfast hope in Him. The desire for these things would come through His Spirit's indwelling presence and work in our lives. Lest we forget, saints of old have determined that the chief end of man is to "know God and enjoy Him forever!" Mercifully, a loving God guides it all.

Here's some Old Testament prophecy concerning the New Covenant, including Ezekiel's:

"I will give you a new heart and put a new spirit within you; I will take the heart of stone out of your flesh and give you a heart of flesh. I will put My Spirit within you and cause you to walk in My statutes, and you will keep My judgments and do them" (Ezekiel 36:26-27).

" 'The day will come,' says the Lord, 'when I will make a new covenant with the people of Israel and Judah. . . . But this is the *new covenant* I will make with the people of Israel on that day,' says the Lord. 'I will put my law in their minds, and I will write them on their hearts. I will be their God, and they will be my people' " (Jeremiah 31:31 and 33)(Emphasis added.)

Simply stated, the New Covenant is the promise God makes to humanity whereby He pledges to forgive sin and restore fellowship with those whose hearts are turned toward Him. Jesus Christ is the mediator of the New Covenant, and His death on the cross is the basis of the promise.

On the occasion of the Last Supper, Jesus spoke of the New Covenant. In Luke 22:20, we read, "Likewise He also took the cup after supper, saying, 'This cup is the new covenant in My blood, which is shed for you.' " Jesus was referencing what would be accomplished by shedding His blood when He died on the cross. Remember, the remission of sins has always demanded a blood sacrifice. That's why millions, perhaps billions of animals, were sacrificed at the Temple. These sacrifices merely covered sin. Jesus was the perfect Passover lamb without sin, without blemish, and without spot. Only His sacrifice forgave sin. Consequently, when Jesus died on Calvary, the wrath of God was satisfied, and all sin debt paid in full - forever - past, present, and future. Rejoice! Jesus' death ended the eternal consequences of sin, too! It was the greatest gift. Salvation is God's gift to humanity through His Son Jesus for all who believed.

Lesson 20: Paul's Closing Summation
Romans 15:1-33

Day Three: **Receive**. Review Romans 15:1-33

Memory Verse: "Now may the God of peace be with you all. Amen" (Romans 15:33).

1. From Romans 15:14, we find that Paul was confident that the brethren were:

   a._____

   b._____

   c._____

2. In Romans 15:15, what has Paul received from God?

3. Review Romans 15:16. Paul's call had a purpose. What was it? Record Romans 15:16 as your response.

4. Review Romans 15:17. What did the things that pertain to God cause Paul to do?

5. Review Romans 15:18-21. Paul was charged with a mission to proclaim the gospel of God.

In a word, who was Paul's primary target? _____

♥ Heart-Check For Today

6. Thinking biblically, what does it mean to "minister," and what's its origin? Have you recently ministered to someone? Or, has God recently used someone to minister to you? Answer the most appropriate question in the space below.

7. Review Romans 15:19. "In mighty signs and wonders, by the power of the Spirit of God,..." Paul had preached. Where? Complete the verse below.

8. From Romans 15:20, why did Paul "aim to preach the gospel, not where Christ was named..."? Thinking biblically, why would this be important?

9. In Romans 15:22, Paul concludes the work of the ministry had hindered him from coming to Rome.

   a. Who was behind this delay: _____

   b. Review Romans 15:23-24. We can see that Paul had a plan but was trusting God for the outcome. What was Paul's plan? Briefly summarize verses 23 and 24 below.

   v. 23 _____

   V. 24 _____

10. Read Romans 15:25. We see that once again, Paul had not been released to go. Why was he further detained? Be specific.

11. Read Romans 15:26-27. What had occurred in Macedonia and Achaia, and to whose benefit? Provide a brief overview.

12. What was the mission? The answer is found in Romans 15:28. Read and complete the passage below.

"Therefore, when I have performed this and have sealed to them this _____, I shall go by way of you to Spain" (Romans 15:28).

13. Paul had a plan, but how did he desire to come? Read and record Romans 15:29 below.

Romans 15:29 –

Paul's ministry desires were bathed and saturated in prayer, as we shall see in the closing passages of this chapter. So much so that he solicited prayer from the saints in Rome. What a leadership model for us. As we prayerfully make plans that advance God's kingdom, we should commit them to God in prayer. As we pray and seek God's "go and guidance," we should invite others to partner with us in prayer. We should be specific in our requests so that we are praying for God's best and direction in unity. Paul told them precisely what he desired. Paul knew that God would either open or close the door. He would be content, either way, knowing and trusting fully in the God whom he believed.

14. Read and review Romans 15:30-32. Paul needed prayer. He invited the Romans to partner with him in prayer. Paul begged the brethren... "through the Lord Jesus Christ, and through the love of the Spirit, that you strive together with me in prayers to God for me..." (on my behalf)

Paul invites prayer for four specific things in Romans 15:31-32. Please list them below. Be specific.

a.

b.

c.

d.

15. What is Paul's concluding benediction in Romans 15:33? Complete the verse below.

"Now the _____ of _____ *be* with you all. Amen" (Romans 15:33).

Lesson 20: Paul's Closing Summation
Romans 15:1-33

Day Four: **Reflect**. Prayerfully Review Romans 15:1-33

Memory Verse: "Now may the God of peace be with you all. Amen" (Romans 15:33).

Paul was on a mission from God, and nothing, even prison, would prevent him from remaining faithful to his call. The gospel reached many while Paul sat in chains because he never lost sight of the Kingdom, His purpose, or God's call. We, too, are on a mission from God. Acts 1:8 declares that we are to be His witness. Rejoice! If you are saved, you are called!

Paul's mission took him many places, but the work always beings at home. It is unlikely that God would call you to a foreign land if you had not yet submitted to His work at home. We are to bloom by His grace and for His glory wherever we are planted. For most of us, our mission begins each day at the breakfast table, surrounded by those we love. And, if you live among non-believers, this may prove to be hostile ground. Yet, our families and those closest to us, like neighbors and colleagues, must be reached with the gospel. That's why we are to live a life that exalts His name by bringing the cross of forgiveness and God's love and mercy into every situation. We are to speak God's truth in love and declare the wonders of our great God and King Jesus at all times.

In other words. what we confess with our mouths must be witnessed and demonstrated through our lives. If we say we are forgiven, we must forgive. If we say that God does not condemn us, we must not condemn. If we say that Jesus is love, we must love all others with abandon. If we say a kind word turns away wrath, we must have a kind word, etc. Within our homes, the authenticity of our transformed lives must prevail. God doesn't save us just to go to heaven. His plan involves us bringing others with us.

To that end, pray for a kingdom vision like Paul's. Pray for bold love that is genuine and sincere. Pray for the salvation of the lost daily, including your family. Lastly, we must pray that our service(s) will be effective right where we're planted.

1. Paul desired for many years to travel to Rome to minister. Do you have the desire to go "some place" to share the gospel? If so, you are invited to share.

2. Read, review, and record Proverbs 16:9 below.

   Proverbs 16:9

3. Read and record Acts 16:7 below.

   Acts 16:7

4. According to the above passages, who is in control? In your words, summarize the message in Proverbs 16:9 and Acts 16:7.

5. Have you ever been prevented from some particular area of service or travel by God? If so, you are invited to share.

6. From Romans 15:23, we see that in Paul's opinion, his work was complete. Therefore, he set his sights on a trip to Spain, which would provide an excellent stop-over before going to Rome. But, things did not come about as he had planned. Thinking biblically, why do you think Paul was hindered?

7. Nonetheless, Paul would remain faithful to his mission and God's plan. We don't get to choose when and where God will use us. The work is God's, and it is birthed in us and springs from us as a result of prayer, fellowship, and intimacy with Jesus. What a wonderful model for ministry work and Christian living, in general. God has a plan, and we don't get to see the fullness of the tapestry that He is weaving. Some go here, and others He sends there, all with a unique purpose and by His divine design! It's important to remember that initially, Paul's desire was to minister to His own - the Jews – but, as you may recall, God said no. As a result, Paul was called to minister among the Gentiles instead.

Read and record Acts 9:15-16 below to discover God's words to Paul through His servant Ananias at the laying on of hands and Paul's sending. Note this occurred immediately following Paul's conversion on the Road to Damascus. If you are unfamiliar with Paul's conversion, the entire story is found in Acts 9.

Acts 9:15-16

v. 15

v. 16

8. God doesn't always send us where we desire to go. Our focus must never be where rather who! God's work of salvation is God's work wherever you are. Although Paul wanted to travel to Rome for many years, he had responsibilities elsewhere, and God hindered his plan. We can make plans,

but we must commit them to God and allow the Holy Spirit to guide us forward or not! He did it for Paul, and He will do so for us.

Are you satisfied to remain where you are until God gives you the "go"? Remember, where He guides, He provides. It is a blessed thing to be found in God's perfect and pleasing will. To be outside of that ideal is a dangerous thing. God doesn't desire just good or better for you; He wants what is best for you instead. Indeed, God's plan is ideal for your life.

Romans 12:2

9. Paul's desire to go elsewhere did not hinder his faithfulness to serve God. In fact, Paul planned to go to Spain (See Romans 15:24), although there is no record in history that this desire ever became a reality. We must never let our desires frustrate God's work at the moment. To long for what God has not given to you is covetous, which is sinful. The 10th commandment says from the New Living Translation, "You must not covet your neighbor's house. You must not covet your neighbor's wife, male or female servant, ox or donkey, or anything else that belongs to your neighbor." In a broader sense, we can covet anything, including the work of the ministry. Have you ever longed for ministry work that God has not given you? If so, you are invited to share.

10. Each day is a gift from God that we will never get back. To focus on tomorrow makes today seem trivial and meaningless. We frustrate God's work for today when we fixate on tomorrow. Is this an area of concern for you? Yes _____ or no_____?

11. The first and most important trait of a leader is humility. Christ was a humble servant, and He is our example.

James 4:10

As we draw this lesson to a close, remember that Abraham and Sarah waited twenty-five years for Isaac, the child of promise. Thankfully most of us don't have to wait so long for God's answers and plans to be revealed. Are you currently waiting on God for the salvation of a family member or friend, for healing, for finances and provision, for strength and love in your marriage, or direction for the next step? Trust Him! He is faithful. We must pray that we don't sin in the wait. A humble servant waits upon the Lord and is satisfied.

A believer trusts in God. That's what faith is. An excellent biblical definition of faith would be *confident obedience to God's word despite the circumstances or consequences.* Do you have this faith? If not, ask God to grow your faith. That's a prayer He always answers in the affirmative. Rejoice! Then trust Him to grow your faith. Sweet sister, in the days and years to come, a marvelous journey of faith is in store for you.

12. Read the prayer below and if you agree, sign and date the page appropriately. Let this serve as a reminder that you have pledge to trust in God's plan for your life. To that end, you will yield wholeheartedly.

Today I asked Jesus to grow my faith and use me as He sees fit. I have laid my plans, desires, and agenda at the foot of the cross. Moving forward, I plan to have no plan. Instead, it's my heartfelt desire to bloom where I'm planted and serve you (Jesus) faithfully each day by God's grace and for His glory. Help me, Oh God, to do so without regret, neglect, or complaining! Give me a heart of joy and satisfaction as I embrace your will. Thank you, Jesus! Amen and Amen.

Date:

Lesson 20: Paul's Closing Summation
Romans 15:1-33

Day Five: **Respond.** Review Romans 15:1-33

Memory Verse: "Now may the God of peace be with you all. Amen" (Romans 15:33).

1. Paul needed prayer and asked for it in Romans 15:30-32. He was in the midst of a spiritual battle. Much hostility arose from those in Jerusalem who had rejected the faith. Paul knew that their hostility might escalate to violence, so he solicited prayer from the believers in Rome. This request reveals Paul's humility, which is the opposite of pride. Paul was inviting brothers and sisters in Christ to join him as he travailed and labored in prayer. Have you ever asked for prayer? How was your request received? Were the united prayers fruitful?

2. Paul knew that adversity and opposition awaited him in Jerusalem. The Spirit had warned him. Remember, Paul was on a mission from God, and even thoughts of what awaited him in Jerusalem did not alter his course or change his focus. Read and review Acts 20:22-24 and complete the passage below.

"And see, now I go _____ in the_____ to Jerusalem, _____ _____ the things that will happen to me there, except that the _____ _____ testifies in every city, saying that _____ and _____ await me. But none of these things _____ me; nor do I count my life _____ to myself, so that I may finish my race with _____, and the _____ which I received from the _____ _____, to testify to the _____ of the grace of God" (Acts 20:22-24).

3. Review the verses above and **_underline_** Paul's mission. **_Circle_** the words that reflect who commissioned Paul.

4. Review Romans 15:30. Paul has named each member of the trinity in this passage. Record the verse below and **_underline_** each member of the trinity that Paul has identified.

Romans 15:30 -

5. In Romans 15:30, Paul mentions the "love of the Spirit." This phrase references Paul's love of the Spirit rather than the Spirit's love for Paul. Do you have love and fellowship with God's Spirit, which is "at home in you?" Do you practice His presence and rest in His guidance? Yes _____ or no _____?

6. That love and fellowship that Paul enjoyed with the Spirit produced faithfulness and obedience. His Spirit will do so in us as well. He seals God's Word in us and brings it to performance in our lives. The fruit is always the same. What's that? It's always faithful obedience! As a result, Paul did not hastily head to Rome or Spain. He was content to wait on God's release to go instead. Can you recall a time when the love of the Spirit prevailed by realigning you with God's Word and His plan or purposes?

7. Paul was not fearful on his behalf; instead, it was the gospel, God's work of salvation, and the sufferings within the church among the faithful that most burdened Paul's heart. Paul was an *intercessor*. Define "intercessor" below.

intercessor:

8. Notice from Romans 15:30 that Paul links believers together. Do you see the link? What is it?

9. There is power in prayer! Most of the work of any ministry is accomplished on our bended knees in prayer. One Bible scholar suggested the work of the ministry is merely the clean-up that follows effectual prayer. Paul knew and understood the power of unity in steadfast, devoted prayer. Read and record Matthew 18:19 below.

Matthew 18:19 –

10. Paul had a job to do in Jerusalem and beyond. To that end, he would remain faithful. In Romans 15:31, Paul desired *"something"* about his service. What was it? Why would this be necessary? Be specific.

11. Paul desired three crucial things in Romans 15:32, and he prayed to that end. What were they specifically?

That I may:_____

by:_____

and may be:_____

12. The joy that Paul referenced in Romans 15:32 was not linked to his circumstances. What was it related to, and what does it mean?

13. Have you been able to experience real joy in crisis, turmoil, or chaos? If so, for the encouragement of others, please share a brief testimony.

14. Paul passes "the peace" of God in Romans 15:33, stating specifically, "Now the God of peace be with you all." That is the final benediction of chapter 15. Paul has already made two profound statements concerning the character and nature of God.

The first one referenced the God of patience and comfort. Identify the verse? _____

Next, Paul referenced the God of hope. Identify the verse? _____

♥ Heart-Check For Today

15. Paul's prayer was to all who believe in the God of salvation – the one true and living God. Do you know the God of patience, comfort, hope, and peace as your personal savior? If you have any doubt concerning your salvation, please seek counsel from your Bible study leader or pastor without delay. God desires that you come to saving faith! Jesus loves you; He died for you!

Note: If you underline your bible, underline these descriptive phrases that express the nature and character of God. The benedictions are found in Romans 15:4-5, 15:13, and 15:33. For encouragement in the days ahead, you may need to recall Paul's description of the One who loves you, died for you, and has called you to saving faith.

Words of Jesus
"Jesus said to them, 'My food is to do the will of Him who sent Me, and to finish His work' " (John 4:34).

Lesson 21: Paul's Commendation, Greetings & Doxology
Romans 16:1-27

Day One: **Read**. Prayerfully Read Romans 16

Memory Verse: "The grace of our Lord Jesus Christ be with you all. Amen" (Romans 16:24).

1. Review Romans 16:1-2 and answer the following questions. Be specific. Use the phrases from verses 1 or 2 in your response.

   Who did Paul commend? v. 1

   How does he describe her? v. 1

   How was she to be received? v. 2

   What did Paul request on her behalf? v. 2

   On what basis does he make his appeal? v. 2

2. From Romans 16:3; 4, who risk their own necks for Paul's life?

_____ _____

3. In Romans 16:3-5, Paul sends greetings to fellow workers. Review verses 16:3-5. List everyone that Paul greets.

4. From Romans 16:3-5, who had a home church?

5. Read and review Romans 16:5-13. Although Paul had not traveled to Rome, he had many friends there. For each name listed below, record Paul's identifying comments for each one.

Epaenetus v. 5 -

Mary v. 6 -

Andronicus and Junia v. 7 -

Amplias v. 8 -

Urbanus v. 9 -

Stachys v. 9 -

Apelles v. 10 -

Aristobulus v. 10 -

Herodion v. 11

Narcissus v. 11

Tryphena and Tryphosa v. 12

Persis v. 12

Rufus v. 13

6. Each named believer in this chapter identifies our former brothers and sisters in Christ and fellow workers for the benefit of the gospel in Rome. God's Spirit has granted Paul the esteemed honor of naming them through the inspired text. For all eternity, they will be recognized as fellow workers, co-laborers for the harvest. Each name listed accompanied, facilitated, or supported those who spread the good news or gospel of Christ in Rome. Because all people matter to God, please record the nine names from Romans 16:14-15 below.

Note: Bible scholars are confident that Rufus, identified in Romans 16:13, was not Paul's natural brother. Instead, Rufus' mother, the wife of Simon of Cyrene, at some time had cared for Paul during his ministry travels.

_____

_____

_____

_____

_____

_____

_____

_____

_____

7. Paul gives a specific instruction in Romans 16:16. Read and record the verse below and explain why this would be necessary? What is Paul hoping to achieve through his request?

Romans 16:16 –

I believe this is necessary because:

Thinking biblically, I believe Paul is hoping:

8. Now it's your turn. First, prayerfully select a believer and record their name below. That could be a parent, grandparent, teacher, pastor, missionary, neighbor, roommate, etc. Next, add a descriptive comment which would identify them to others. Note: Please do not say: "Suzy with red hair and three kids." Instead, share about their Christian character and nature. In your opinion, what sets them apart from all others within the body of Christ? We are much more than a name. All of us bring something unique to the family of faith. Remember, each of us is created on purpose and for God's divine purpose. Lest we forget, God has done amazing things in and through His global church – including us/you! You are invited to share.

9. In closing, spend some time praying for your local church, the persecuted church, missionaries (at home and abroad), and those who labor faithfully in peril, famine, and much hardship by God's grace and for His glory. We are called to be His witness, and laborers are necessary to spread the gospel message. Jesus has said, the harvest is ripe, but the workers are few! Lastly, pray for workers for the harvest!

Read and review Paul's words from Romans 10:14-18 below before you pray.

"How then shall they call on Him in whom they have not believed? And how shall they believe in Him of whom they have not heard? And how shall they hear without a preacher? And how shall they preach unless they are sent? As it is written: 'How beautiful are the feet of those who preach the gospel of peace, Who bring glad tidings of good things!' But they have not all obeyed the gospel. For Isaiah says, 'Lord, who has believed our report?' **So then faith comes by hearing, and hearing by the word of God.** But I say, have they not heard? Yes indeed: 'Their sound has gone out to all the earth, And their words to the ends of the world.' " (Romans 10:14-18) (Emphasis added.)

Lesson 21: Paul's Commendation, Greetings & Doxology
Romans 16:1-27

Day Two: **Research**. Review Romans 16

Memory Verse: "The grace of our Lord Jesus Christ be with you all. Amen" (Romans 16:24).

I. Using a bible, bible dictionary, or concordance define the following **key words.**

commend v. 1 -

helper v. 2 -

firstfruits v. 5 -

divisions v. 17 –

II. Read the following **key phrases.**

holy kiss v. 16 - Paraphrasing from *Smith's Bible Dictionary,* a "holy kiss" was the widespread custom of greeting among men in the ancient western Mediterranean. It was also the custom in ancient Judea. The holy kiss greeting was widely practiced among Christians. Keep in mind. Among the Jews - a greeting kiss was not only a common practice - it was anticipated and expected.

The "holy kiss" is still observed as the official greeting of warmth and unity between Jews, particularly among the orthodox and ultra-orthodox, even to this day. The "kiss" conveys *shalom*, which means *peace*. It was an outward symbol of an inward embrace of the heart, which implied passing the peace. It was akin to saying, "May God's peace be with you."

In the New Testament, a holy kiss is also referenced by Peter as the kiss of love. Among believers, it was a kiss of peace, which symbolized Christ-centered unity, devotion, and love for one another.

Remember, we are one in Christ! Five examples of the "holy kiss" are found in the New Testament. Four appear in the writings of Paul and one in Peter's epistle. (See1 Peter 5:14.) Paul is not making a simple suggestion in verse Romans 16:16, and the Romans would know his meaning. They were being **commanded** to greet one another with genuine love, unity, and sincerity of heart. Please note: In each occurrence, the "holy kiss" was a command from the original language.

Let's analyze the verse. The command is *"greet,"* ***aspazomai*** - it's the **what** of the verse. The verb appears in the imperative mood in the aorist tense, which presents the verb's action as a "snapshot" event. In other words, the verbal action is portrayed simply and in a summary fashion, without respect to any process, delay, or thought. In this case, it (the greeting – the "holy kiss") was to flow naturally from the heart – as the heart's expression. There was no outside influence affecting the performance of the verb other than the command to perform it.

The **who** of the verse is *"one another or your brothers' (or sisters'), believers,"* and the **how** is with a "holy kiss." That defines the way the greeting was to be carried out. **It is important to note that men greeted only men in this fashion, and women greeted women, likewise.** It would be forward and inappropriate for women to greet men with a "holy kiss" and vice versa.

Why was the kiss regarded as holy? Generally speaking, believers are called to a life of holiness. That means a life dedicated, devoted, and consecrated (set apart) for God and His purposes. This implication here is that we desire transformation and yield to sanctification toward holiness. The results? Over time, we grow more and more like Jesus. Someone who looks like Jesus displays a posture or attitude of love with the accompaniment of moral and spiritual excellence. Hence, we want to be conformed to His image and yield to His Spirit's work within us. Although no believer is perfect, the heart is in view. A desire to live our life to the glory of God should inspire our journey to "live with the purity of mind, thought, and body in view." All of which is undergirded by love because God has first loved us. Paul said believers are to offer themselves as holy sacrifices – literally, a living sacrifice - in Romans 12:1. The mutual service of love for God and love for others would be expressed, affirmed, demonstrated, and sealed through the "holy kiss."

Too, the "holy kiss" was a greeting that signified Christ-centered unity and agape love among the brothers and sisters in Christ. (Remember, unlike brotherly love - a.k.a. philia love), the essence of agape love is goodwill, benevolence, and willful delight in the object of that love. Agape love involves faithfulness, commitment, and an act of the will. It is distinguished from the other types of love by its lofty moral nature and strong character. Agape love is sacrificial love, which asks nothing in return. Paul highlighted the essence of its beautiful nature in 1 Corinthians 13.) If you are unfamiliar with these verses, you may want to review them now.

Therefore, the "holy kiss" would be especially welcomed by new believers who were often estranged from family or outcasts because of their faith. To be accepted and embraced by the family of faith would be encouraging and precious to them, indeed.

St. Augustine, a well-known 4th-century philosopher, and believer had said, "This is a sign of peace; as the lips indicate, let peace be made in your conscience. That is, when your lips draw near to those of your brother, do not let your heart withdraw from his. Hence, these are great and powerful sacraments."

Nineteenth-century American theologian Albert Barnes noted the following while reflecting on the "holy kiss" of Romans 16:16. "The use of the word 'holy' here serves to denote that Paul intended it as an expression of 'Christian; affection; and to guard against all improper familiarity and scandal.' " He further concluded that the "holy kiss" was not only a common practice for the early Christians but it was also practiced in their religious assemblies.

Read and complete 1 Peter 5:14 below.

"Greet one another with a _____ of _____" (1 Peter 5:14).

Here are other examples from Paul's writings.

"All the brethren greet you. Greet one another with a holy kiss" (1 Corinthians 16:20).

"Greet one another with a holy kiss" (2 Corinthians 13:12).

"Greet all the brethren with a holy kiss" (1 Thessalonians 5:6).

obedience to the faith v. 26 - Authentic saving faith always produces obedience and submission to Jesus Christ. Believers must trust Him, love Him, and obey Him. Jesus said faith produces obedience.

John 14:15 –

Lesson 21: Paul's Commendation, Greetings & Doxology
Romans 16:1-27

Day Three: **Receive**. Review Romans 16

Memory Verse: "The grace of our Lord Jesus Christ be with you all. Amen" (Romans 16:24).

1. In Romans 16:17, Paul gives a warning to the brethren. Read and review the verse and, in your own words, outline Paul's warning.

2. Thinking biblically, why would Paul's warning be important to the church in Rome or any church?

3. According to Romans 16:18, who do these divisive individuals serve, by what method, and to whose detriment? For your response, use the words from the passage.

4. What has been known to all concerning the brethren from phrase one of Romans 16:19?

5. Read and record the remainder of Romans 16:19 below. Essentially, Paul instructed them to keep watch. What was Paul's concern?

6. Review Romans 16:20. What does Paul promise the God of peace will accomplish through them as a result?

7. Paul passes the peace in the last phrase of Romans 16:20. What word is missing from this passage, and what does it mean? Note: This verse echoes Paul's greeting in Romans 1:7.

"The _____ of our Lord Jesus Christ *be* with you. Amen" (Romans 16:20).

8. Prayerfully review Romans 16: 21-23. Thankfully, Paul doesn't have to labor alone. Neither do we. All over the world, members of "the body" serve in numerous ways, by God's grace and for His ultimate glory. It's the work of Christ's church since the beginning, and we all play a part. What work? It's believers co-laboring with Christ, as His Spirit so directs, to advance God's king-

dom. From verses 21-23, who served, and in what capacity? Match the names of column two with the description provided by Paul from each passage in column one.

my fellow worker	Gaius
my countrymen	Quartus
why wrote (penned) this epistle	Timothy
Paul's host	Erastus
host of the entire church	Timothy
city treasurer	Lucius, Jason, & Sosipater
a brother	Tertius

9. Again, what is extended from Romans 16:24? _____

10. Complete the missing words from Paul's closing benediction in Romans 16:25-27.

"Now to _____ who is able to establish _____ according to my _____ and the _____ of _____ _____, according to the _____ of the mystery kept secret since the world began but now made _____, and by the prophetic _____, made known to all _____, according to the _____ of the everlasting _____, for obedience to the _____ -" (Romans 16:25-26).

11. Read and review Romans 16:27 and answer the following. (For your response, complete the passage from the following questions.)

    a. to who?

b. how is He alone described?

c. through who?

Lesson 21: Paul's Commendation, Greetings & Doxology
Romans 16:1-27

Day Four: **Reflection.** Prayerfully Review Romans 16

Memory Verse: "The grace of our Lord Jesus Christ be with you all. Amen" (Romans 16:24).

Paul's greetings in Romans 16 have great significance even though the named saints have been deceased for centuries. Not to oversimplify the obvious, but people matter. Jesus died to save people, and Paul ministered to reach people. The gospel message is for people!

Although we are flawed and frail, people are the pinnacle of God's creation. We are His crowning glory. Everyone who exists was created and called into existence by a triune God before the foundation of the world. Take note. He made everything to fulfill His plan and purpose. That would include all of humanity, even folks like Pharaoh and Judas, etc. We are created in the image of God, and although we may not be aware of it, we were created with a deep need for God and a longing to know, discover, and enjoy fellowship with our Creator.

Being Connected.

That's why people must be our priority. We see this conveyed through all of Paul's New Testament writings. By the time Romans 16 is written, Paul has successfully preached from Jerusalem to Illyricum, according to Romans 15:19. His work there is now complete, and he desires to travel to Rome. He was on a mission from God and had the vision to share the gospel throughout the world. Paul was progressive, a forward thinker, and the gospel message burned within him. He desired not to build upon another man's foundation, but he would go whenever and wherever God called. It was his intense desire to reach as many people as possible - in every corner of the world - as God would so permit, guide, and provide.

As you might imagine, Paul was a busy man with responsibility in many places, yet, from a close review of Romans 16, it appears that Paul took the time to know people. Paul has not sent a blanket greeting to Rome, for Paul has identified 29 people within this text. Why? Because people matter to God, and they mattered to Paul. His cares and concerns for others were genuine. These named individuals are known, loved, and appreciated by Paul.

Keep in mind, many of these listed were people that Paul had never met face to face. He did not have access to Facebook, the internet, telephone, Skype, IM, text, or any countless number of electronic resources available to make "connecting" with people easy. Mail delivery was difficult, and vast distances often separated Paul from others because transportation was a slow and tedious event involving the foot, the camel, or the boat. Most importantly, Paul waited on God to move him from place to place.

Nonetheless, Paul made it his business to be connected with people. He made it his business to let them know how much he cared for them - personally and spiritually. Paul prayed for them and told them so. He was a great source of strength, encouragement, and inspiration to those who labored near and far. So in the future, when it comes to caring for the family of faith, may we be inspired and follow Paul's lead.

1. Paul was not journeying through life alone, and neither are you. Prayerfully make a list of those who are in your sphere of influence.

2. Thinking biblically, how might you faithfully demonstrate God's love to them?

3. Do you remember them in prayer? Yes _____ or no_____? If no, why not?

4. Have you recently been encouraged by a brother or sister in Christ? If so, you are invited to share.

5. Ministry flows both ways. How have you most recently encouraged another brother or sister in Christ? You are invited to share.

6. The call of pastors, teachers, and missionaries is weighty! Their service or preparation for it may require separation from home and family. It happens, and not for isolation-sake, but their development and equipping to reach the lost. Sometimes, before they ever "go far," they are separated through a season of preparation – for study, prayer, language, and cultural training, and other preparedness. Is it worth it? Absolutely! Nonetheless, the absence is real, and the enemy loves to use it to discourage the goers and those left behind. Will you commit to pray for those who labor on the frontline and their families? There is no greater service we can give. When I served on the foreign mission field, the prayers of family and friends meant more to me than their financial support. Although God used the combination mightily, we coveted their prayers!

Yes, I will pray for:

Date:

♥ Heart-Check For Today

7. In closing, you are invited to extend a word of thanks and encouragement to those who labor in your local church and community. Let them know, like Paul, that their work is making a difference. Reach out and tell them that you are praying for God's anointing, provision, and blessings over their lives and call. A simple word of thanks goes a long way to encourage the faith of others. Paul got this. He understood it personally. When you extend your words of thanks, make it personal. Be sure to let them know how their labors have affected your life and encouraged your faith.

8. You are invited to write a short prayer of thanksgiving below for the persecuted church. Don't forget to include those who live in peril and endure hardships for the benefit of the gospel.

Lesson 21: Paul's Commendation, Greetings & Doxology
Romans 16:1-27

Day Five: **Respond.** Review Romans 16.

Memory Verse: "The grace of our Lord Jesus Christ be with you all. Amen" (Romans 16:24).

Before we respond to God's Word, let's review Paul's warning from Romans 16:17-20.

1. Sometimes, the enemy creeps in, even within the family of faith, Christ's church. Review Romans 16:17. Who should you avoid? Be specific.

2. To fully understand the urgency of Paul's warning, notice the word *"avoid"* in Romans 16:17. The verbal action within this verse is found in the word "avoid." It appears in the imperative mood, which makes it a command. **Avoiding** divisive people was not a mere suggestion. Paul's words did not imply if you feel like it or if it's convenient. He emphatically said, "avoid these folks – period." God commands you! Paul was earnest in his instruction. Record the entire verse below. Underline the last phrase.

Romans 16:17

3. Have you had to avoid "...those who cause divisions and offenses, contrary to the doctrine which you learned..."? (Review Romans 16:17). If so, give a brief testimony of God's faithfulness in light of your obedience.

4. Read and review Proverbs 6:16-19 to recall the seven things that the Lord hates.

   a. List the first six things that the Lord hates below.

   b. Complete the last phrase of Proverbs 6:19 below. Underline the offense.

     "And one:

5. Sometimes, the enemy is within the church. Can you recall when a church you attended was disrupted by someone who had evil plans to divide the body and disrupt church unity? If so, you are invited to share.

6. Review Romans 16:18. How does Paul describe these disruptive individuals? List all the descriptive words below.

God's Word cannot be changed. If you move a millimeter from the truth, it is no longer the truth. It is not to be accompanied by flamboyance or flair - flattery and the like, but preferably with passion, reverence (holy fear), and esteem. Even today, some denominations "stand-up" for the reading of God's Word. So, be on your guard. If someone exhibits flattering speech, smooth-talking, strange behavior, and undiscernible utterances which taut "superior spirituality," as in they've obtained something unique from God that you didn't – be forewarned! This type of self-promotion is not from God! The same Spirit – His Spirit – resides in all of us. He has not withheld anything you need, nor would He.

7. Authentic faith exalts Jesus and points others to Him because that's the work of His Spirit, which is "at home" in all believers. It never draws attention to self. Paul died to self, and like Jesus, his focus was on others and the gospel – the good news - never himself. Simply stated, authentic faith exalts Jesus and is empowered by His love, which reaches outward toward others and never inward to elevate or promote self. Saving faith always says, "God first, others second, and me third." Paul reminds the church at Corinth that God's indwelling Spirit brought forth the Word, empowered the Word, and accompanied the Word unto good works. In other words, there was nothing powerful about Paul, the man, and he said so. In and of himself, Paul was a weak man, just like the lot of us. Let's take a look. Complete 1 Corinthians 2:1-5 below.

"And I, brethren, when I came to you, did not come with excellence of _____ or of _____ declaring to you the testimony of God.

v. 2 For I determined not to know anything among you except Jesus Christ and _____ _____.

v. 3 I was with you in _____, in _____, and in much _____.

v.4 And my _____ and my _____ were not with _____ words of _____ wisdom, but in demonstration of the _____ - and of _____,

v. 5 that your _____ should not be in the _____ of men but in the _____ of God" (1 Corinthians 2:1-5).

8. Read Romans 16:20. Paul gives the assurance of God's everlasting, reliable power, protection, and faithfulness. How is God described?

9. Without using a direct quote, Paul has reached back to the Old Testament scriptures. Read and review Genesis 3:15. Do you see the connection in these verses? If so, list the connection below.

    Romans 16:20   Genesis 3:15

10. Dr. Warren Wiersbe had this to say concerning Romans 16:20. From *Wiersbe's Expository Outlines of the New Testament,* we read, *"It is right for the church to keep an eye on 'church tramps' who run from one church to another, causing trouble and division. These people are smooth talkers and know how to fool the simple, but the discerning saint will see through their disguises. Conquer Satan—don't let him conquer you!"*

Thinking biblically, what would be your best course of action if the time comes when you encounter a "church tramp(s)"? How should you respond? You are invited to share.

11. Paul has concluded this beloved epistle with a benediction that has corresponding similarities to Romans 1:1-11. In his closing words, Paul has highlighted the major themes of the epistle. To conclude our study, read and review Romans 16:25-27 in light of Romans 1:1-11 and respond accordingly. If possible, record a passage from Romans in your response.

   a. God is the one who establishes and strengthens believers.

   b. Through what means is this accomplished?

   c. What is the "good news" message?

   d. In and through who has the "mystery" been revealed? What is the mystery?

   e. What is the objective among all nations?

   f. Who might be forever praised?

Some conservative Bible scholars suggest that Paul began a statement in verse 25 and enthusiastically interrupted his thoughts with supporting facts he had previously outlined in Romans. They assert that Paul's entire thought, if unbroken, would read: "To God who alone is wise (v. 25) be glory forever through Jesus Christ." (v. 27)

According to The Westminster Shorter Catechism, glorifying God and enjoying Him forever is the chief end or purpose of man. As you conclude your Romans study, read Paul's parting benediction of Romans 16:25-27. No doubt, Paul was praising God! You are invited to praise God too!

Praise Him:

1. For God's plan to keep and establish believers.

2. For the gospel, which is the good news revealed in and through Jesus Christ, and for Paul's faith in Him and anointed service to it.

3. For the revelation of "the mystery" that salvation was for the Gentiles and the Jews, as promised through the prophetic scripture.

4. For "the mystery," which is obedience to the faith.

5. For God's glory - forever - through Jesus Christ, our Lord.

Close in prayer.

The Romans Road to Salvation

Romans 3:10
"There is none righteous, no, not one;..."

Romans 3:23
"For all have sinned and fall short of the glory of God..."

Romans 5:8
"But God demonstrates His own love toward us, in that while we were still sinners, Christ died for us."

Romans 5:12
"Therefore, just as through one man sin entered the world, and death through sin, and thus death spread to all men, because all sinned—"

Romans 6:23
"For the wages of sin *is* death, but the gift of God *is* eternal life in Christ Jesus our Lord."

Romans 10:9-11
"...that if you confess with your mouth the Lord Jesus and believe in your heart that God has raised Him from the dead, you will be saved. For with the heart one believes unto righteousness, and with the mouth confession is made unto salvation. For the Scripture says, 'Whoever believes on Him will not be put to shame.' "

Romans 10:13
"For 'whoever calls on the name of the Lord shall be saved.' "

About The Author

Anne is a missionary and a graduate of Metro Atlanta Seminary. She is President of Open Heavens Publishing and its companion nonprofit, which exists for the express purpose of providing biblical curriculum to women in prisons, rehabs, assisted living facilities, and rural churches where economic or physical hardships are demonstrated. Overall, Anne is committed to getting God's Word into the hands of those who are hungry to study but lack provision or resources. Since 2004, she and her husband have remained faithful to their overall mission. Teaching scripture and growing others in faith and practice through the study of God's Word.

Other ministry highlights include outreach to the impoverished, establishing Bible studies in government-funded communities and homeless shelters, facilitating Laundry Love, launching feeding ministries, church planting, and urban city ministry complete with curbside prayer, preaching, and teaching. She and her husband have lived and ministered in four southern states, Mexico and Jerusalem, Israel.

Her more traditional work has included writing, developing, and teaching Bible college curriculum, bible studies, and women's retreats. Additionally, she has served as a women's leader and facilitated countless small groups at home and abroad, as well as trained and mentored women who will serve as wives to tomorrow's pastors and missionaries, should the Lord tarry. Lastly, she has spearheaded prayer ministry and served as a community pastor in mid-town Atlanta.

Anne's life testifies that God's Word transforms hearts, and she desires to share the word with other women. Her love and passion for God's Word and literal approach to scripture, sprinkled with a bit of humor and frankness about the troubling times and circumstances in which we live, is not only challenging and inspiring but clever and refreshing as well. In short, her inspirational teaching encourages women's faith. She's passionate about women trusting in Christ alone as they come to a fuller understanding of God's Word. Through in-depth Bible study, she motivates them to embrace God's Word - wholly - and challenges them to love it, live it, and trust it!

To date, except for her study, *To Rome With Love*, all of Anne's studies and course curriculum feature biblical truths and insights from women of scripture. She has used the rich texts of their lives to shape and develop every lesson - every story. Her straightforward approach to the facts of scripture and her strong faith and hope in God is mixed with heartwarming, true-life missionary takes and adventures, as well as antidotes and confessions from one woman's heart to another. Anne loves all the women of the Bible and hopes you will too! (A complete list of books and studies is available on her website: annenicholsonauthor.com).

After 14 years of full-time missionary service, she and her husband returned to Auburn, Alabama. Their initial call to Auburn in 2004 launched a vibrant college ministry on the university's campus.

To date, former students passionately serve in ministry endeavors worldwide. Anne and Jimmy have a blended family of grown children sprinkled throughout the southeast. They include five sons, one daughter, a daughter-in-law, and three energetic grandchildren - two boys and one girl.

You are invited to contact Anne for information about teaching materials, future publications or solicit her for a speaking engagement, conference, or retreat. She may be reached at womenofthebible01@gmail.com. Her website is: www.annenicholsonauthor.com

www.ingramcontent.com/pod-product-compliance
Lightning Source LLC
Chambersburg PA
CBHW080917170426
43201CB00016B/2180